American Slavery:
A Very Short Introduction

VERY SHORT INTRODUCTIONS are for anyone wanting a stimulating and accessible way in to a new subject. They are written by experts and have been translated into more than 40 different languages.

The series began in 1995 and now covers a wide variety of topics in every discipline. The VSI library now contains nearly 400 volumes—a Very Short Introduction to everything from Indian philosophy to psychology and American History—and continues to grow in every subject area.

Very Short Introductions available now:

Available soon:

For more information visit our web site

www.oup.com/vsi/

Heather Andrea Williams

AMERICAN SLAVERY

A Very Short Introduction

OXFORD
UNIVERSITY PRESS

OXFORD

UNIVERSITY PRESS

Oxford University Press is a department of the
University of Oxford. It furthers the University's objective
of excellence in research, scholarship, and education
by publishing worldwide.

Oxford   New York

Auckland   Cape Town   Dar es Salaam   Hong Kong   Karachi
Kuala Lumpur   Madrid   Melbourne   Mexico City   Nairobi
New Delhi   Shanghai   Taipei   Toronto

With offices in

Argentina   Austria   Brazil   Chile   Czech Republic   France   Greece
Guatemala   Hungary   Italy   Japan   Poland   Portugal   Singapore
South Korea   Switzerland   Thailand   Turkey   Ukraine   Vietnam

Oxford is a registered trade mark of Oxford University Press
in the UK and certain other countries.

Published in the United States of America by
Oxford University Press
198 Madison Avenue, New York, NY 10016

Library of Congress Cataloging-in-Publication Data
Williams, Heather Andrea.
American slavery : a very short introduction / Heather Andrea Williams.
pages   cm. — (Very short introductions)
Includes bibliographical references and index.
ISBN 978-0-19-992268-0 (pbk.)
1. Slavery—United States—History.   I. Title.
E441.W723 2014
306.3'620973—dc23
2013044645

Printed by Integrated Books International, United States of America
on acid-free paper

For the descendants

Contents

Acknowledgments

I am indebted to the numerous historians of the Atlantic slave trade, American slavery, and Reconstruction, whose scholarship is reflected in this book. My sincere thanks to Nancy Toff, my editor at Oxford University Press, and to the readers for the press whose suggestions and insights helped to improve the book. Thanks also to my nephew Clay, my sisters, brother-in-law, nieces and nephews, and to the friends who sustain me. Finally, my gratitude to Prescott Murray for all his support.

List of illustrations

Chapter 1
The Atlantic slave trade

This is how it began

In 1441, one decade before Christopher Columbus was born, a ship left Portugal and headed south in the Atlantic Ocean to the coast of West Africa with orders from Prince Henry to bring back a cargo of seal skins and oils. Prince Henry, also called the Infante or the Navigator, planned to explore Africa and obtain gold and human captives, but because Antam Gonçalves, the ship's captain, was young and inexperienced, Prince Henry sent him to obtain only mundane items. Gonçalves, however, was ambitious; as the ship approached the coast of Mauritania in West Africa, Gonçalves decided to impress the prince by taking back what he knew was his true desire. According to Gomes Eannes de Zurara, the royal librarian who wrote a chronicle of the expedition, Gonçalves suggested to his crew, "Oh how fair a thing it would be if we who have come to this land for a cargo of such petty merchandise, were to meet with the good luck to bring the first captives before the face of our Prince." Then he laid out his plan. When night fell, he and his men would explore the land near the coast in search of inhabitants. With the advantage of the element of surprise, he was certain that his crew would be able to capture one of them to take back to the prince. He expected that the prince would reward him highly.

That night, Gonçalves and his men began their search. They had to travel farther inland than planned, but soon they came across footprints. The crew attacked a man who fought them and ran, but they wounded him with a javelin and captured him. Then they captured a woman. Although he had at first hoped to take one captive, Gonçalves wanted to capture more people the following night so that the prince would not only learn about the people but could also make a profit by selling them. The Portuguese sailors attacked an encampment of Africans, whom they called "Moors." The people fought back, but their spears could not overcome the Portuguese javelins. The crew killed three Africans and captured ten, including a man named Adahu who said he was from a noble family. He had traveled and learned Arabic, and was able to communicate with the Arabic-speaking interpreter the Portuguese had brought along. He promised that if Gonçalves released him he would provide many more slaves in exchange. Although Gonçalves was tempted to make the ransom, he was much more eager to return with his bounty to the prince; he and his men loaded the caravel with the captives as well as the skins and oils they had been sent to gather, and sailed back to Portugal.

This episode marked the beginnings of an era of European exploration that brought the continents of Europe and Africa into contact with one another through forced transatlantic migrations from Africa to Europe, and eventually to the Caribbean and North and South America. In the 1440s Gonçalves and other Portuguese explorers began a process that created an Atlantic world connected in ways that it had never been before. This crisscrossing of trade routes and the introduction of African slaves into a new world shaped the lives and experiences of millions of Africans, Europeans, and Native Americans who met on the shores of America.

Emerging from the devastation of the bubonic plague (Black Death) that killed nearly half of Europe's population, Portuguese ship builders adapted Chinese and Arabic inventions to develop an improved sailing ship. The caravel, with its triangular sail, two masts, and more accurate compasses, allowed sailors to maneuver in the Atlantic Ocean more efficiently, enabling them to successfully undertake much longer journeys. The caravel, along with cartographers' and mathematicians' improved understanding of winds and currents, made it possible for explorers to navigate from Portugal in the south of Europe, down the coast of North Africa, to West and Central Africa. More importantly, they could move through the currents and winds and thus make their way back to Europe.

To be sure, Europeans and Africans had practiced slavery for centuries. In ancient Europe slavery was common in the Roman Empire, but the institution declined for economic and political reasons between the fifth and eighth centuries C.E. when European countries developed systems of semifree serfdom instead. With the expansion of Islam in the eighth century C.E., Muslim merchants carried on a thriving trade of mostly women and children from sub-Saharan Africa to North and East Africa, the Mediterranean Islands, and Spain. Muslim traders relied on having a steady supply of captives from conquered lands. At the same time, Italian merchants carried out a slave trade in which they sold people from Slavic countries (including Armenia, Bulgaria, and Russia) to purchasers in the Mediterranean and in what is now called the Middle East. So prevalent was this Italian-operated slave trade that the word "slave" was derived from the word "Slav," a name for people from Slavic countries.

In part due to conflicts between Muslims and Christian Europeans over Muslims' enslavement of Christians, many medieval European societies came to believe that Christians should not enslave other Christians. In the 1440s as they tested their ship-building and sailing skills and traveled to Africa in search of goods, Portuguese rulers began to take Africans as slaves. To their thinking, these captives—because they were black—were not Christians and were therefore prime subjects for enslavement. Portugal was a small, poor country. Prince Henry and other leaders wanted to acquire wealth by obtaining gold from the west coast of Africa and by competing with Arab traders who traveled to India for spices and traded slaves from sub-Saharan Africa to North Africa and Europe.

Slavery had also existed in much of Africa in some form, but it usually did not constitute the largest source of labor. People generally became slaves by being captured during wars, in raids on enemies, or as punishment for crimes. For the most part, slaves worked in domestic roles, and some performed religious roles or worked in agriculture, though some worked on large plantations or in mines. In African societies slavery was not a fixed institution; for example, the child of a free father and an enslaved mother could become a free member of society. Sub-Saharan Africans had been sold to Arab traders for centuries, and the arrival of the Portuguese in the 1400s intensified the trade in slaves, increased the number of places from which people would be captured, and changed the types of labor that slaves would perform.

When Antam Gonçalves presented his captives to Prince Henry, Adahu, the captured nobleman, made a direct plea to the prince to be ransomed. He said he could provide not only other captives as replacement but also information about distant lands that the Portuguese might explore and capture. Henry agreed and provided Adahu with clothing. According to the chronicler, Adahu "was very well clad in garments given him by the Infant who considered that, for the excellence of his nobility that he had above the others, if he received benefits, he would be able to be of profit to his benefactors by encouraging his own people and bringing them to traffic." Prince Henry was correct in this assessment and upon returning to Africa, in exchange for his own freedom, Adahu provided the Portuguese sailors with "ten blacks, male and female."

More expeditions followed as even some of those Portuguese who had at first opposed exploration and the slave trade began to praise the practice of capturing Africans. According to the chronicler, "as they saw the houses of others full to overflowing with male and female slaves, and their property increasing, they thought about the whole matter, and began to talk among themselves." Thus the trade expanded with Portuguese men sailing to the African coast for the express purpose of attacking African villages and capturing people. The chronicler wrote of one such expedition in the 1440s: "Then you might see mothers forsaking their children, and husbands their wives, each striving to escape as best he could. Some drowned themselves in the water; others thought to escape by hiding under their huts; others stowed their children among the sea-weed, where our men found them afterwards, hoping they would thus escape notice." On this particular occasion, the Portuguese managed to capture 165 men, women, and children, and thanked God for being on their side. They packed the people into ships, and many died from disease, starvation, and confinement before they ever reached Europe.

In 1444, after such a voyage to Guinea in West Africa, a group of caravels landed in Lagos, Portugal, with its cargo of people. Leaders of various enterprises gave accounts of their exploits to the visiting prince Henry. The captain then made a suggestion regarding what should be done with the Africans: "Because of the long time we have been at sea...as well as for the great sorrow that you must consider they have at heart, at seeing themselves away from the land of their birth, and placed in captivity, without having any understanding of what their end is to be—and moreover because they have not been accustomed to a life on shipboard—for all these reasons are poorly and out of condition; wherefore it seemeth to me that it would be well to order them to be taken out of the caravels at dawn, and to be placed in that field which lies outside the city gate, and there to be divided into five parts, according to custom, and that your Grace should come there and choose one of these parts, whichever you prefer."

The captives were sick, anxious, and weary, but the divisions were made, and the prince received his royal fifth, a tithe of sorts, consisting of forty-six people. The remaining people were divided among those who had either participated in the capture or financed the expedition. Some of these men kept their captives, others sold them as slaves. This public display of African captives caused great excitement among the people of Lagos, and more of them came to support Henry's investment in explorations as they began to think that they too could benefit from having slaves.

In contrast to the excitement of the Portuguese, the division and sale in Lagos was an emotional event for the captives. "What heart," the chronicler wrote, "could be so hard as not to be pierced with piteous feeling to see that company? For some kept their heads low and their faces bathed in tears, looking one upon another; others stood groaning very dolorously, looking up to the height of heaven, fixing their eyes upon it, crying out loudly, as if asking help of the Father of Nature; others struck their faces with the palms of their hands, throwing themselves at full length upon the ground; others made their lamentations in the manner of a dirge, after the custom of their country. And though we could not understand the words of their language, the sound of it right well accorded with the measure of their sadness.... [T]o increase their sufferings still more, there now arrived those who had charge of the division of the captives, and who began to separate one from another, in order to make an equal partition of the fifths; and then was it needful to part fathers from sons, husbands from wives, brothers from brothers. No respect was shown either to friends or relations, but each fell where his lot took him."

As those captured wept in anticipation of being separated from their families and the people they knew, the chronicler expressed sympathy for the people who were torn from their family members, but the prince and others in Portugal "reflected with great pleasure upon the salvation of those souls that before were lost." Within a few years, Portugal became a slave-owning society as the demand for slave labor increased, and slave ownership came to be regarded as a status symbol that rulers held up as a matter of pride to foreign visitors. By 1455, 10 percent of Lisbon's population consisted of Africans.

The chronicle of the voyages of Portuguese sailors to Africa brings into sharp focus the origins of what became an extensive centuries-long trade in African people to Europe, South America, and North and Central America. The narrative also raises many of the issues and gives a sense of the tensions or contradictions that arose when Europeans delved into an Atlantic slave trade. First, Europeans, including the Portuguese, had, for the most part, ended slavery by the 1440s, but with new access to Africa the Portuguese still captured people and took them against their will to Portugal to work. Next, they claimed that God blessed the Portuguese when they prevailed over the Africans who attempted to fight them off; God, they claimed, was on the side of the Portuguese. Moreover, they employed Christianity as a justification for capturing people and taking them to Europe. The sailors thanked God for helping them to subdue their "enemies," even though these Africans had not initiated contact or conflict, and had only resisted being attacked and captured. Prince Henry asserted that the captives in Portugal would be better off because their souls would be saved through Christianity, and he thought it his duty as a Christian to evangelize and take the message of Christ to the so-called infidels and pagans. Early on, those who participated in the Atlantic slave trade employed Christianity, a religion that arguably promoted a gospel of liberation, to justify enslaving others. This Christian justification of the enslavement of Africans continued as long as slavery lasted in the Americas.

There was also the matter of collusion or collaboration of some Africans with Europeans in the slave trade. Adahu stands in here for other African leaders who participated in the slave trade or permitted it to take place in their jurisdictions. At first sailors physically attacked and captured people, but as time went on and

Africans resisted capture, the Portuguese employed other strategies. On one of the early expeditions sailors exchanged cloth for a woman and indeed could have purchased more people had the crew taken more goods with them. These early exchanges foreshadowed what became common practice during the transatlantic slave trade. As the Portuguese and other Europeans expanded their desire for slaves, they entered into arrangements with African rulers who allowed African traders to go inland to capture people whom they marched to the coast and traded with waiting Europeans for India-produced cotton textiles, porcelain from China, rum, tobacco, weapons, gunpowder, iron for making tools, cowry shells used as currency, and other items. Some African rulers negotiated with Europeans and imposed duties or taxes on the trade, made demands regarding the goods they wanted as payment, and benefitted from systems of gift-giving.

These rulers did not think of themselves as Africans or as black people; their identities instead derived from being members of a specific village or an ethnic group. Therefore, they did not sustain a sense of unity with, or loyalty to, captives from other groups. In fact, people were generally captured in wars with other groups that increased in frequency as African traders obtained weapons from Europeans. And as Europeans captured more and more land in the regions of the New World, the demand for slave labor to cultivate sugar cane, tobacco, and other crops increased, which meant that African traders now reached far beyond the Atlantic coast, deeper inland.

The Middle Passage

When Christopher Columbus made his Spanish-funded journeys in the 1490s to the Caribbean and North and South America, he opened up mineral-rich and fertile lands on which European countries planted their flags and the Christian cross. Portugal had led the way, but by the 1500s and 1600s others, including the Dutch, the Spanish, the French, the Danes, and the English, began

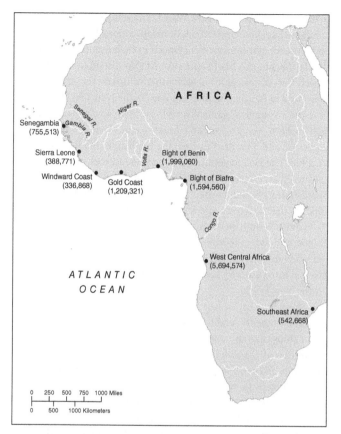

1. Map of major coastal regions from which captives left Africa, all years. The numbers shown here are estimates of the numbers of slaves taken from each region. Africans captured in the interior of the continent departed on ships for the months-long journey across the Atlantic Ocean.

to exploit Africa and the New World. The jealousies, rivalries, and conflicts that characterized relationships among these countries on the European continent continued in their excursions to Africa, the Caribbean, and North America. As they jostled for wealth and power, Europeans captured each other's ships on the Atlantic, their forts in Africa, and their colonies in the New World. Over time the Portuguese claimed Brazil; the Spanish claimed Jamaica, Bolivia, Peru, Venezuela, Cuba, Mexico, and Florida; the Dutch, Suriname and New Amsterdam; the English, Barbados and Virginia. The violent conflicts among these European powers continued as, for example, the English captured Jamaica from the Spanish in 1655 and wrested New Amsterdam from the Dutch in 1665. In the Caribbean and South America, colonists forced indigenous people including the Arawaks, Caribs, Mayans, Tainos, and Aztecs to mine gold or silver or to plant sugar cane, but when most of the native people died from overwork or disease, Europeans looked to Africa as the source of labor for the New World.

In the seventeenth, eighteenth, and nineteenth centuries, much larger ships than the original Portuguese caravels made the Atlantic crossings that became known as the Middle Passage, with slave ships packed with an average of three hundred people each. Approximately 35,000 voyages took captives from Africa to Europe and the Americas from the 1500s to the 1860s. The number of people transported changed over time as the demand for slave labor increased in North and South America, reaching its peak in the late 1700s. Scholars estimate that between the sixteenth century and the 1860s, 12, 520,00 captives, one-quarter of whom were children, left African ports in Senegambia, Sierra Leone, the Windward Coast, the Gold Coast, the Bight of Benin, the Bight of Biafra, West Central Africa, and Southeast Africa.

Before departing, most captives lived for months in dark and claustrophobic dungeons also called "slave castles," such as Elmina in Ghana on the Gold Coast. Portuguese traders built the Elmina

Twenty-five-year period	Number of Africans who embarked on slave ships
1501–25	13,363
1601–1625	352,843
1651–75	488,064
1701–25	1,088,909
1776–1800	2,008,670
1801–25	1,876,992
1826–50	1,770,979
1851–66	225,609

Excerpted from the Transatlantic Slave Trade Database. http://www.slavevoyages.org/tast/assessment/estimates.faces

fortress in 1482 to store gold, but it eventually became a space for holding captives until ships were ready to sail to the Caribbean, South America, or North America. Despite the cannons built onto the top of the fortress, the Dutch captured Elmina from the Portuguese in 1638. In 1653 Swedish traders built a nearby fortress that also faced the Atlantic Ocean, but the Danes eventually captured it, and one year later in 1664 the English took control, naming it Cape Coast Castle. Like Elmina, Cape Coast Castle initially stored goods—gold and timber—but it too became a dungeon that held African captives.

The people held in those dungeons came from families and communities. Each of them had stories of love and fear and loss, but most of those stories are lost to us. Still, a few survive. Ottobah Cugoano, for example, recalled that he was playing in the woods with other children when strange men with cutlasses and guns kidnapped them. When the men separated Cugoano from his

2. **Major regions where captives disembarked, all years. The numbers shown here are estimates of the number of slaves that landed in each region. Europeans took millions of African captives to labor in numerous locations in South and North America, the Caribbean, and Europe.**

friends, he was so despondent that he refused to eat or drink. His captors took him to the coast where they sold him for a gun, a piece of cloth, and some lead. He was taken to Cape Coast Castle where he saw his "countrymen chained to one another, two by two until a boat came and took them to a larger ship." Samuel Crowther told a story of being captured in Nigeria when he was about fifteen years old. He was sold several times, he said, once for a horse, once for tobacco and rum, and once for cowry shells. He attempted suicide but ended up in the coastal town of Lagos, Nigeria, where he saw white men for the first time. "Having no more hope of ever going to my country again, I patiently took whatever came…although it was not without a great fear and trembling that I received, for the first time, the touch of a White Man, who examined me whether I was sound or not." The men and boys, Crowther wrote, were tied together with a chain about six feet long, with an iron fetter on the neck of each individual, and fastened at both ends with padlocks. This arrangement was particularly excruciating for the boys who suffered when any of the men pulled the chain in anger or to find a more comfortable position for sleeping. The boys were often bruised, and they feared suffocating from the tightness of the fetters as well as the lack of fresh air inside the dungeon. Crowther spent four months in that dark, stifling space.

After months in the slave castles, captives squeezed, one by one, through the low, narrow, "Door of No Return" and climbed into waiting canoes that took them to larger ships. Other people bypassed the slave dungeons and went directly to the ships, where captains inspected and purchased them. John Newton, an Englishman, captained such a ship that sailed from Liverpool to the Windward Coast of Africa in the 1750s. He kept a journal documenting his days spent at sea and those spent on the coast of West Africa purchasing people brought to him by African traders. He examined people's bodies and determined their value, and then placed the purchased ones on his ship to sail to the Caribbean or Charleston in South Carolina. Much later, after renouncing the slave trade, Newton wrote a pamphlet in support of the abolition movement. He reflected on the conditions in which captives lived on the English slave ships: "With our ships the great object is, to be full. When the ship is there, it is thought desirable she should take as many as possible. Their lodging rooms below the deck, which are three (for the men, the boys, and the women), besides a place for the sick, are sometimes more than five feet high and sometimes less; and this height is divided towards the middle, for the slaves to lie in two rows, one above the other, on each side of the ship, close to each other, like books upon a shelf. I have known them so close that the shelf would not, easily, contain one more. And I have known a white man sent down, among the men, to lay them in these rows to the greatest advantage, so that as little space as possible might be lost." Newton recalled the difficulties for the people packed in this way and chained in irons to move their hands or feet, and it was harder still to get up or to lie down without experiencing pain.

Alexander Falconbridge, the surgeon on one of the English slave ships, spent much of his time below the deck examining and treating captives while the ship was on the coast of Africa being loaded over a period of months, and also while the ship sailed for another two months or so to the Caribbean or North America. According to Falconbridge, captives "were frequently stored so close as to admit of no other posture than lying on their sides." The height between the decks was so low that adults could not stand erect. The crew sometimes took these chained people onto the deck during the day to exercise to the beating of a drum or the bottom of a tub. In an act of resistance to their condition of captivity, some people refused to eat, but crew members forced them, sometimes threatening to burn them with hot coals if they did not swallow. Like Newton and Crowther, Falconbridge commented on the lack of sufficient ventilation below deck where the rooms were "intolerably hot." As a result of having too many people in cramped quarters, lack of ventilation, anxiety on the part of the captives, and inexperience with being at sea, many people became ill on the ships, often from seasickness, scurvy, small pox, and intestinal diseases such as dysentery. In one instance Falconbridge described the floor of the deck where the captives lived as "being so covered with blood and mucus it resembled a slaughterhouse. It is not in the power of the human imagination to picture to itself a situation more dreadful or disgusting. Numbers of the slaves having fainted, they were carried upon deck, where several of them died, and the rest were, with great difficulty, restored." The situation was gruesome indeed, Falconbridge recalled that the "surgeon, upon going between decks in the morning to examine the situation of the slaves, frequently finds several dead; and among the men, sometimes a dead and living negroe fastened by their irons together. When this is the case, they are brought upon the decks, and being laid on the grating, the living negroe is disengaged, and the dead one thrown overboard."

The ships sailed to Europe, Brazil, Mexico, Peru, Barbados, Jamaica, Cuba, Berbice, Haiti and the Dominican Republic, Charleston, and New Orleans, taking people who would work as miners, cowboys, seamstresses, cooks, and sailors; and others were sold to labor in fields of sugar cane, tobacco, indigo, rice, or coffee, producing the cash crops that European investors and colonists demanded. They came from places in West Africa that are today the countries of Sierra Leone, Liberia, the Ivory Coast, Ghana, Togo, Benin, Nigeria, Cameroon, as well as from West Central Africa and Southeast Africa. And they spoke numerous languages including Mandinka, Bambara, Wolof, Akan, Twi, Yoruba, Fon, and Kikongo.

More than 12 million Africans boarded the ships, but nearly 2 million died during the Middle Passage and found their final resting place at the bottom of the Atlantic Ocean. Approximately 10,700,00 disembarked. Of those who survived, only about 5 percent went to North America, most of the rest went instead to South America and the Caribbean. Although only a small percentage of the African captives arrived in the area that became the United States, over time they came to constitute a large proportion of the country's foreign-born population. Indeed, before 1820, four times as many Africans as Europeans lived in the colonies and states. It took some time, but as European countries, particularly England, colonized the lands that became the United States, they relied more and more on the labor of captive Africans and their descendants.

Chapter 2
Putting slavery into place

America held promises of wealth and freedom for Europeans; in time, slavery became the key to the fulfillment of both. Those who ventured to the lands that became the United States of America arrived determined to extract wealth from the soil, and they soon began to rely on systems of unpaid labor to accomplish these goals. Some also came with dreams of acquiring freedoms denied them in Europe, and paradoxically slavery helped to make those freedoms possible as well. As European immigrants to the colonies initiated a system of slavery, they chose to enslave only those who were different from them—Indians and Africans. A developing racist ideology marked both Indians and Africans as heathens or savages, inferior to white Europeans and therefore suited for enslavement. When continued enslavement of Indians proved difficult or against colonists' self-interest, Africans and their descendants alone constituted the category of slave, and their ancestry and color came to be virtually synonymous with slave.

Although Europeans primarily enslaved Africans and their descendants, in the early 1600s in both northern and southern colonies, Africans were not locked into the same sort of lifetime slavery that they later occupied. Their status in some of the early colonies was sometimes ambiguous, but by the time of the American Revolution, every English colony in America—from Virginia, where the English began their colonization project, to Massachusetts, where Puritans made claims for religious freedom—had people who were considered lifetime slaves. To understand how the enslavement of Africans came about, it is necessary to know something of the broader context of European settlement in America.

In the winter of 1606, the Virginia Company, owned by a group of merchants and wealthy gentry, sent 144 English men and boys on three ships to the East Coast of the North American continent. English explorers had established the colony of Roanoke in Carolina in 1585, but when a ship arrived to replenish supplies two years later, the colony was nowhere to be found. The would-be colonists had either died or become incorporated into Indian groups. The English failed in their first attempt to establish a permanent colony in North America. Now they were trying again, searching for a place that would sustain and enrich them.

By the time the English ships got to the site of the new colony in April 1607, only 105 men and boys were left. Despite the presence of thousands of Algonquian-speaking Indians in the area, the leader of the English group planted a cross and named the territory on behalf of James, the new king of England. They established the Jamestown Settlement as a profit-making venture of the Virginia Company, but the colony got off to a bad start. The settlers were poorly suited to the rigors of colonization. To add to their troubles, the colony was located in an unhealthy site on the edge of a swamp. The new arrivals were often ill, plagued by typhoid and dysentery from lack of proper hygiene. Human waste spilled into the water supply, the water was too salty for consumption at times, and mosquitoes and bugs were rampant. No one planted foodstuffs. The colonists entered winter unprepared and only gifts of food from the Powhatan Indians saved them.

In the winter of 1609/10, a period that colonist John Smith called the "starving time," several of the colonists resorted to cannibalism. According to Smith, some of the colonists dug up the body of an Indian man they had killed, boiled him with roots and herbs, and ate him. One man chopped up his wife and ate her. John Smith feared that the colony would disappear much as Roanoke had, so he established a militarized regime, divided the men into work gangs with threats of severe discipline, and told them that they would either work or starve. Smith's dramatic strategy worked. The original settlers did not all die, and more colonists, including women and children, arrived from England to help build the struggling colony.

The first dozen years of the Jamestown Colony saw hunger, disease, and violent conflicts with the Native People, but it also saw the beginnings of a cash crop that could generate wealth for the investors in the Virginia Company back in England, as well as for planters within the colony. In 1617, the colonist John Rolfe brought a new variety of tobacco from the West Indies to Jamestown. In tobacco the colonists found the saleable commodity for which they had been searching, and they shipped their first cargo to England later that year. The crop, however, made huge demands on the soil. Cultivation required large amounts of land because it quickly drained soil of its nutrients. This meant that colonists kept spreading out generating immense friction with the Powhatan Indians who had long occupied and used the land. Tobacco was also a labor-intensive crop, and clearing land for new fields every few years required a great deal of labor. The colony needed people who would do the work.

Into this unsettled situation came twenty Africans in 1619. According to one census there were already some Africans in the Jamestown colony, but August 1619, when a Dutch warship moored at Point Comfort on the James River, marks the first documented arrival of Africans in the colony. John Rolfe wrote, "About the last of August came in a dutch man of warre that sold us twenty Negars." According to Rolfe, "the Governor and Cape

Marchant bought [them] for victuals at the easiest rates they could." Colonists who did not have much excess food thought it worthwhile to trade food for laborers.

The Africans occupied a status of "unfreeness"; officials of the colony had purchased them, yet they were not perpetual slaves in the way that Africans would later be in the colony. For the most part, they worked alongside the Europeans who had been brought into the colony as indentured servants, and who were expected to work usually for a period of seven years to pay off the cost of their passage from England, Scotland, Wales, the Netherlands, or elsewhere in Europe. For the first several decades of its existence, European indentured servants constituted the majority of workers in the Jamestown Colony. Living conditions were as harsh for them as it was for the Africans as noted in the desperate pleas of a young English indentured servant who begged his parents to get him back to England.

In March 1623, Richard Frethorne wrote from near Jamestown to his mother and father in England begging them to find a way to get him back to England. He was hungry, feared coming down with scurvy or the bloody flux, and described graphically the poor conditions under which he and others in the colony lived. He was worse off, he said, than the beggars who came to his family's door in England. Frethorne's letter is a rare document from either white or black servants in seventeenth-century Virginia, but it certainly reflects the conditions under which most of them lived. The Africans, captured inland, taken to the coast, put on ships, taken to the Caribbean, and captured again by another nation's ships, were even farther removed from any hope of redemption than Frethorne. Even if they could have written, they would have had no way of sending an appeal for help. As it happens, Frethorne was not successful either. His letter made it to London but remained in the offices of the Virginia Company. His parents probably never heard his appeal.

Life in the early Virginia colony was difficult for both white and black laborers, but the sources suggest that the possibility of full freedom existed for both. Slavery was not yet firmly in place, and the population of Africans and African Americans remained low, not exceeding 5 percent, for the first four decades. Some of this first generation may have spent time in the Caribbean or on ships among Europeans before arriving in Virginia. They had varying levels of experience interacting and negotiating with Europeans, and they brought those skills to bear on their existence in America. They have been called Atlantic Creoles to denote their familiarity with European cultures.

Anthony Johnson, sold into Jamestown in 1621, two years after those first twenty Africans arrived, gives a sense of the possibilities for Africans in the colony. Johnson was enslaved, yet his owner allowed him to farm independently, likely at least in part to thank him for his services during a war with Indians. Approximately twenty years after entering the colony, Johnson gained his freedom, and ten years later received 250 acres of land through headrights, a system in which the colony granted land, usually to white men, to encourage settlement in the colony. Under this system, an individual received a specified number of acres of land for each person he brought into the colony, including family members and slaves. Johnson's sons also received several hundred acres of land. It took Johnson twenty years to gain his freedom, much more than the seven years a white indentured servant would have served. Nonetheless, he managed to become a successful planter, even owning slaves and suing successfully for the return of a man whom Johnson claimed was his slave but who claimed he was an indentured servant who had served more than his time. A small number of other free blacks lived near Johnson, but by the time he obtained land, the majority of black people in the colony were slaves.

Farther up the Atlantic coast Dutch settlers obtained the island of Manhattes from local Indians in 1626 and named it New Amsterdam, but these colonists had a difficult time enticing others to leave economic prosperity in the Netherlands to join them in the New World. As a result, a large percentage of the early settlers came from other European countries including England, France, Germany, and Ireland, but potential settlers were frightened away by constant conflicts between the Dutch colony, Indians, and the English. In 1626, the same year the colony was settled, the Dutch West India Company brought in eleven slaves, all African men, who did much of the work of building the infrastructure of the colony. The company eventually brought in African female laborers as well to become wives to the men, and it allowed the men to own goods, earn wages, and petition the courts to settle disputes with whites. The Dutch even armed these men to help fight Indians. The men, realizing their importance within the colony, negotiated for a status of half-freedom for themselves and their wives in which they continued to be owned by the Dutch

3. Beginning in 1626, enslaved Africans worked to build the infrastructure of Dutch New Amsterdam. The colony later became English-controlled New York.

West India Company but could work for themselves when not needed. At first this more privileged category of unfreeness applied only to those first eleven men and their wives, not to their children. Eventually about sixty other people gained admission to the category of half-freedom.

Farther north, slavery existed as well. In Massachusetts where the Pilgrims landed at Plymouth in 1620 and where Puritans settled in the Massachusetts Bay Colony in 1630, those who had left Europe in search of freedom to practice Christianity as they saw fit had few apparent qualms about enslaving fellow humans. In his sermon on the ship *Arabella* on the Atlantic on the way to Massachusetts, John Winthrop, governor of the colony, laid out his belief in social hierarchies in which there would be rich people and poor people, and neither group would challenge the other. According to Winthrop, "the riche and mighty should not eate up the poore nor the poore and dispised rise up against and shake off their yoke." It was incumbent upon each group to maintain a status quo of unequal social and economic status. Winthrop thought that he and fellow Puritans were undertaking a mission blessed by God and that they should act according to the law of God as others would look to them as a model. "For we must consider that we shall be as a city upon a hill," he said, "the eyes of all people are upon us. So that if we shall deal falsely with our God in this work we have undertaken, and so cause him to withdraw his present help from us, we shall be made a story and a by-word through the world. We shall open the mouths of enemies to speak evil of the ways of God." Winthrop thought slavery consistent with the laws of God; its practice would not bring on the wrath of God.

During the seventeenth century, the number of enslaved Africans in Massachusetts was never large. However, the insidious reach of the slave trade did not elude the colony as a number of Massachusetts merchants became wealthy by participating in the Atlantic slave trade as ship builders, and through a web of Atlantic world economic relationships that spanned Europe, Africa, America, and the Caribbean.

In Massachusetts, as in Virginia, New York, and South Carolina, colonists enslaved Native Americans as well as Africans. Often they sold Indians captured in wars into slavery in the West Indies, but they kept some, particularly women and girls, to labor among them. In 1637, for example, John Winthrop informed the Plymouth Plantation governor, William Bradford, that colonists and Pequots had fought, and the colonists had slain or captured about seven hundred natives. According to Winthrop, the colonists beheaded the leaders and divided up the prisoners. They sent the male children to Bermuda with William Pierce, and doled out the women and girls to work in several towns in the colony. In February 1638, Winthrop noted in his journal the arrival of captive blacks who had been obtained in exchange for the Indians. Pierce had also purchased cotton, tobacco, and salt. Later, in the 1670s, Massachusetts colonists again shipped Indians to the West Indies as slaves during King Philip's War. At the end of the 1600s approximately twelve hundred Native Americans, most of them women and girls, were enslaved in Massachusetts in places that later became synonymous with American liberty, such as Concord, Walden, and Boston. Winthrop himself owned some of these slaves, as did other prominent Puritans including Cotton Mather, the well-known minister.

Just as it did in parts of Africa, the European demand for slaves motivated some Indians to engage in wars in order to capture people for sale into slavery. By the mid-1600s there was a thriving Indian slave trade in Virginia and South Carolina; here some Indian groups traded Indian captives for goods including guns. But engaging in the trade of Indians often held negative consequences for colonists, including vulnerability to attack as well as the possibility of jeopardizing their trade of commodities, such as deerskin, with some Indian groups. By the end of the seventeenth century, although South Carolina continued to hold some Indians in slavery, or to trade them to Virginia or the Caribbean in exchange for horses and cattle, the trade in Indians greatly diminished. In New York, the main concern was retribution from other Indians. In 1679 the colony made it illegal to enslave any member of the Indian groups that lived within the colony, but the law provided that Indians could remain slaves if they had been enslaved elsewhere and were brought into the colony. In 1706, the colony outlawed the enslavement of Indians altogether and provided that "Negroes alone shall be slaves." It was difficult to enslave Indian men for long on lands they had occupied and knew well, or if they had allies nearby. It was much less complicated, though more expensive, to bring in Africans, new to the region, who had no home to which to run or relatives to bring about retribution.

In the mid-seventeenth century, as colonists became more dependent upon unpaid labor, they began a process of putting slavery into place formally through legislation and court rulings. By so doing, they aimed to eliminate the ambiguous condition of Africans and African Americans, and to a lesser extent, Native Americans, and thus clarify any fuzzy notions of "unfreeness." These laws articulated divisions between blacks and whites—or "Christians" as whites were often called—with whites held up as superior beings who diminished themselves by associating with blacks. Elites in the colonies, those who put the laws into place or issued the judgments of the courts, expressed a desire to keep blacks and whites apart socially even though the two groups often labored under similarly oppressive conditions. By the end of that century black people were being held in lifelong, hereditary slavery, meaning that they, their children, and their grandchildren's children would be enslaved. No longer could they expect to work for a period of time and gain their freedom. Colonists in Virginia, Massachusetts, Dutch New Amsterdam, or English New York did not establish a system of perpetual slavery all at once, but at the end of the century, slavery was firmly in place: Africans and their descendants were clearly demarcated as the enslaved.

An early expression in law of presumed white superiority came in 1630 in the *Judicial Proceedings of the Governor and Council of Virginia*. The record reads: "September 17th, 1630—Hugh Davis to be soundly whipt, before an assembly of negroes and others for abusing himself to the dishonor of God and shame of Christianity, by defiling his body in lying with a negro; which fault he is to acknowledge next Sabbath day." The court considered the woman below the social station of Hugh Davis because of her race; Davis was punished by a public whipping to humiliate him and to send a message to blacks and whites that interracial sex would not be tolerated. Of course the laws could never completely keep people apart, as evidenced in a 1640 case in which Robert Sweat, a white man, was ordered to do public penance at a church for impregnating a black woman. Still, the colony conveyed its disapproval of these interracial relationships and asserted the claim that black people were inferior to whites.

In 1640 Virginia armed "all persons except negroes." By law, white men had an obligation to defend the colony from attacks by Native Americans or Europeans, but it was too risky to arm people who were being made into slaves. In that same year, the court in Virginia issued a ruling that again pointed out the ways that black people were to be treated, and it revealed one process by which blacks were being made into slaves. In the case of John Punch, three indentured servants, Victor, from the Netherlands, James Gregory, from Scotland, and Punch, a black man, escaped together from their master. They made it to Maryland, but once captured, they were taken back to Virginia where the court ordered that each one should "receive the punishment of whipping and to have thirty stripes apiece." The court ordered Victor and Gregory, the two white men, to add one year of service to their master when their indenture expired, and then serve the colony for three additional years. In other words, each of them would serve for four years beyond the time of his original indenture. But then the court made a different ruling for the third runaway, providing "that the third being a negro named

John Punch shall serve his said master or his assigns for the time of his natural Life here or elsewhere." The court ordered Punch to be locked into a lifetime of servitude to his master or anyone his master decided to give or sell him to. Furthermore, the court stated clearly that this much harsher sentence accrued because Punch was black.

As Virginia ambled toward lifetime slavery for Africans and African Americans, Massachusetts led the way by being the first colony to enshrine slavery into the law. The Massachusetts Puritans, who sought freedom for the expression of their religious beliefs, also believed that slavery was biblically endorsed. Unlike in some other colonies, though, Puritan ministers including Cotton Mather advocated for what they considered the biblically ordained treatment of slaves. Mather pointed to the Apostle Paul, who urged a fellow Christian to treat his slave as a brother. It is not surprising then, that when the Massachusetts legislature embraced slavery in laws called The Body of Liberties, it invoked both Christianity and God. The law of 1641 reads as follows: "There shall never be any bond slavery, villenage or Captivity amongst us unless it be lawful Captives taken in just wares, and such strangers as willingly sell themselves or are sold to us. And these shall have all the liberties and Christian usages which the law of god established in Israel concerning such persons doth morally require. This exempts none from servitude who shall be Judged thereto by Authority." Puritans held to a stricture against "man-stealing," meaning that they approved slavery as long as people were not stolen, or more likely, so long as the Puritans did not have to *know* that they were stolen. And, as Mather urged, the law imposed a moral obligation to treat slaves as brothers, as prescribed in the New Testament.

In the latter part of the seventeenth century, other colonies including Virginia and its neighbor Maryland; New York, which came under English rule in 1664; Connecticut; and South Carolina, settled by Barbadian colonists in the 1670s, designed laws to establish and regulate slavery. In 1662 Virginia adopted a law that made slavery hereditary and declared that the status passed through the mother, rather than through the father as would have been the case in England. The Virginia law read, in part, "Whereas some doubts have arisen whether children got by any Englishman upon a negro woman should be slave or ffree. *Be it therefore enacted* that all children borne in this country shalbe held bond or free only according to the condition of the mother." This law acknowledged that though it was illegal, interracial sex continued to occur, and slave owners wanted to ensure that the offspring of their female slaves would not be automatically free simply because their father was a white man. The law had the effect of enabling the white owner of an enslaved woman to claim his own children as his slaves. Although this law was specific to the children of interracial contacts, the policy of matrilineal enslavement applied to all children. It was much simpler to determine the mother of a child than the father, and this provision made it easy for the slave owner to identify his property whether the child was the offspring of a white man, a free black man, or of a black man who belonged to a different owner.

Virginia and other colonies also took steps to resolve any thought that conversion to Christianity could exempt Africans or African Americans from slavery. Because the English had long held that one Christian should not enslave another, colonists feared that enslaved people would try to escape through a religious loophole. Dutch colonists in New Amsterdam suspected the same thing, and in 1655 the Dutch church stopped converting Africans to Christianity, claiming that they were not sincerely pious but simply wanted to free their children from being slaves. In Virginia in 1667, the legislature made clear that baptism would not exempt children or other enslaved people from slavery. Owners, the legislation said, could feel perfectly free to offer the blessed sacrament of baptism to their slaves as this would not alter their condition of enslavement.

In 1669 Virginia enacted a law that said it was not murder for an owner to kill a slave while punishing him. The logic was that because time could not be added to the service of people who were already slaves for life, sometimes only violence could correct obstinate behavior; if such violence resulted in the death of the slave, then so be it. The law assumed that an owner would never intentionally kill his slave and thus destroy his own property, and therefore he could not have the requisite intent to sustain a charge of murder. Black people were being locked into a condition of perpetual slavery, as some of them were resisting their owners, the law provided protection for owners who endeavored to exercise control over the people they now owned.

Indeed, control loomed large in the minds of slave owners and legislatures. In Virginia, whites could own blacks and Indians but those two groups could not own whites. To prevent insurrections, enslaved people were required to have written permission from their owners or overseers to leave their property. If any black person or slave "presumed to lift up his hand in opposition against any Christian," that person would be whipped on the bare back. In Maryland, interracial marriage was made a crime because the children of a black father and a white mother caused a great deal of confusion as slave owners were beginning to have grave concerns about being able to identify who was black and could, therefore, be enslaved. Maryland later passed an act that described marriages between black men and white women a "disgrace not only of the English but also of many other Christian nations." Maryland law also severely punished white women who had children with black fathers, and Virginia prohibited all interracial liaisons denouncing the offspring as "that abominable mixture and spurious issue." When the English took over the New York colony, they freed those people who had been half-free but put in place laws that mimicked the Virginia laws, thus rendering slavery for other Africans and African Americans hereditary and perpetual.

Through legal rulings and legislation it is possible to see slavery and racism growing up together. As black people were being turned into lifetime slaves, the people in power separated them out for different treatment and did so in ways that debased them. The iedology of white supremacy had taken hold. Interracial relations were a disgrace to the English and other Christian nations, but not to Africans. As the debasement of black people increased, the position of white servants improved, because they could now distinguish themselves from those who were performing some of the same work but who had black skin. Still, white indentured servants remained the majority of the labor force.

With slavery in place as a legal institution, and Africans and their descendants identified as the people to be enslaved, in 1676 Bacon's Rebellion exploded on the Virginia landscape and resulted in increased dependence on slavery instead of on indentured servitude. The rebellion arose out of class tensions between white indentured servants and the elite men in the colony. Opportunities were worsening in the 1670s for servants as the legislature passed more repressive laws aimed at protecting wealthy, propertied men. Prospects for those near the end of their indenture grew smaller; a white male servant could not automatically hope to become a landowner. Frustrations grew, and more and more servants ran away. In 1673 William Berkeley, governor of the colony, said of the white servant class, "Six parts of Seven at least are Poore, Indebted, discontented, and Armed." He feared that if the colony were attacked by another European country, most of the men would join with the invaders in hopes of gaining access to more land and wealth.

In the summer of 1676, Nathaniel Bacon harnessed the anger of these young white men who resented their exclusion from the dream of tobacco wealth. Aligned with them were free black men and black men who realized that their own options had diminished dramatically. Bacon was not himself a poor man; in fact, he belonged to the gentry and had arrived in Virginia from England a few years earlier and Governor Berkeley had appointed him to the council. Still, Bacon and his supporters wanted more access to land and accused Berkeley and the colonial government of failing to seize land from the local Indian groups. The governor insisted that he would honor the colony's treaties with the Indians. Angered, Bacon and his men massacred hundreds of Occaneechi Indians, then went to Williamsburg where they stoned the governor's house. They marched on Jamestown and burned the colony's capital to the ground. The uprising created panic and terror in Virginia. In October 1676 Bacon died of dysentery, and the arrival of armed ships from England quelled the violence.

In the aftermath of the rebellion, the divide between slavery and freedom became even wider. In colonial Virginia wealthy planters created a new order that dramatically reduced their reliance on white indentured servants and increased their dependence on black slave labor. The English government began investigating the treatment of indentured servants, and gradually planters brought in fewer servants from England and other parts of Europe. Some of the white former servants, now freemen, gained more access to land in Virginia while some began to colonize territories in Kentucky and Carolina. These moves helped to siphon off former servants' tensions. The rebellion also had a dramatic impact on Native Americans as hundreds, perhaps thousands, died at the hands of Bacon and the rebels. Others were driven out of Virginia into what is now Kentucky and Tennessee where they encountered pressure from whites moving into those territories.

With the plantation revolution that resulted from the rebellion, the nature and pace of work for enslaved black people changed radically. As the importation of English servants declined, so the importation of African slaves increased. The number of slaves in Jamestown grew from three thousand in 1680 to thirteen thousand in 1700 and twenty-seven thousand in 1720. Over the course of the seventeenth century, Virginia evolved from a society with slaves to a slave society where the major form of labor was slavery and all the slaves were black. By the end of the century, slavery was also in place in other colonies and along with it the racial distinctions that diminished blacks and elevated whites. As European servants gained freedom, more and more Africans and African Americans became trapped into lifetimes of forced labor.

Chapter 3
The work of slavery

By the end of the seventeenth century, through ideology, laws, and practice, the American colonies had put slavery into place. A century and a half later, when James Henry Hammond delivered his "mudsill" speech to the U.S. Senate in 1858, he therefore drew upon a long history to defend the system of slavery that had transformed him from economically middling into a wealthy man. "In all social systems there must be a class to do the menial duties, to perform the drudgery of life. That is, a class requiring but a low order of intellect and but little skill," said the senator, planter, and former South Carolina governor. "Its requisites are vigor, docility, fidelity. Such a class you must have, or you would not have that other class which leads progress, civilization, and refinement." This class of workers, Hammond asserted, "constitutes the very mud-sill of society and of political government, and you might as well attempt to build a house in the air, as to build either the one or the other, except on this mudsill. Fortunately for the South, she found a race adapted to that purpose to her hand. A race inferior to her own, but eminently qualified in temper, in vigor, in docility, in capacity to stand the climate, to answer all her purposes. We use them for our purpose...and call them slaves." It took white southern elites until the nineteenth century to develop such a full-throated defense of slavery, but Hammond's perspective on forced labor reflected how white slave owners had long thought about African Americans.

In this worldview, wealthy white men did the thinking; black people did the work.

Enslaved people did indeed perform much of the drudgery that built the wealth of the colonies and, later, the American nation. The first eleven enslaved men in Dutch New Amsterdam and those who subsequently joined them laid down the physical infrastructure of the colony. They belonged to the Dutch West India Company and did its bidding to develop the colony: They built the roads, cleared land, cut down trees to produce lumber for buildings and wood for fires, and they burned the lime used in outhouses and for burials. They also tended livestock and raised crops for the colony on farms the company owned. In 1660 when Peter Stuyvesant, governor of the colony, requested that the Dutch West India Company provide more slaves for the colony, he described the physical attributes he sought and the type of labor the men would perform. "They ought to be stout and strong fellows," he said, "fit for immediate employment on this fortress and other works; also, if required, in war against the wild barbarians, either to pursue them when retreating, or else to carry some of the soldiers' baggage." By barbarians, Stuyvesant meant Native Americans, and Dutch colonists did in fact arm enslaved Africans to fight against Indians. When the English seized control of the colony in 1664, the reliance on slave labor only increased: mid-eighteenth-century New York had the largest slave population of any colony north of Virginia, and in the 1770s, at the time of the American Revolution, there were about twenty thousand enslaved people in New York, more than half of them on Long Island where they worked primarily in agriculture.

In most parts of New England, harsh weather and stony soil proved unfavorable to the development of large plantations. These colonies developed economies that included shipping, shipbuilding, fishing, and manufacturing in addition to farming. Given the diversity of the economy, individual enslaved people could be called on to perform a wide range of tasks such as cultivating crops, taking care of animals, working on a printing press, fishing, whaling, or performing domestic labor in the owner's home. Most worked on small family farms, often alongside the owner and his sons, and they raised not one dominant cash crop as in the southern colonies but various crops, as well as livestock and dairy products.

The majority of whites in New England never owned slaves; of those who did, most owned between one and four people. In Rhode Island and Connecticut where the land was more fertile than in northern New England, some farmers owned as many as sixty people. On these larger holdings, slaves worked on farms raising sheep, vegetables, and tobacco, and tended to horses, oxen, and cattle that their owners bred. Robert Hazard of Rhode Island, a wealthy landowner, came close to approximating the large planters of Virginia and South Carolina. In 1730 he owned twelve thousand acres of land and numerous slaves, including twenty-four women and girls who worked in his creamery.

Enslaved people who worked in owners' homes in the North performed a range of duties. Women, in addition to cooking, cleaning, washing, and nursing children, spun wool, weaved, and knitted. Men served as cooks, coachmen, butlers, and valets. Many enslaved men also worked as artisans along with their owners. These men practiced trades including blacksmithing, carpentry, tanning, shipbuilding, and coopering, in which they made the wooden barrels used for storing and transporting goods. In the early colonies, these businesses were usually conducted in the home, but many moved into factories or workshops later on.

So prevalent was enslaved labor in the northern colonies that some white workers felt threatened on two counts. First, they thought they would not be able to compete against the unpaid labor of enslaved people; and second, whites thought their status would be diminished if they performed the same work as slaves, and sometimes that of any black person, free or enslaved.

Distinctions based on race had developed in the colonies early on, and some white workers asserted a claim that they were different from and better than enslaved people. In New York in 1628 white workers objected to the training of enslaved people by the Dutch West India Company to perform skilled labor, and their demands led white officials to proclaim that the black people in the colony were not *capable* of doing skilled work. This is one example of how colonists created a narrative of black inferiority despite the fact that black people had already been performing the tasks. In Boston, enslaved men worked in so many trades that in 1661 white workers lobbied successfully for a law prohibiting the use of black people in the crafts. This does not seem to have changed the practice, however, as slave owners simply kept using enslaved people for whatever purposes they deemed necessary.

Not surprisingly, whites also challenged black people's ability to perform intellectual work. Diminishing their intellect was yet another way to justify enslaving African Americans, and it had the added benefit of preserving some types of work for whites, and creating and maintaining clear social and economic boundaries between blacks and whites. In an explicit challenge to African Americans' intellect, eighteen prominent Massachusetts white men—including John Hancock and Thomas Hutchinson, the governor of the colony—examined Phillis Wheatley in Boston's Town Hall in 1772 to determine whether she could possibly have produced the poetry she claimed to have written.

Wheatley, born on the west coast of Africa, was captured and taken to Boston. In 1761 John Wheatley, a wealthy Boston tailor and merchant, purchased the seven-year-old girl on the wharf in Boston to work as a domestic servant for his wife. In an unusual gesture, the Wheatleys tutored her, and she learned to read and write in English and also became proficient in Latin. Phillis Wheatley began writing poetry at the age of twelve and although local newspapers had published some of her poems, she and the Wheatleys could not raise the necessary funds to publish a book of

4. Brought to Massachusetts from Africa as a child captive, Phillis Wheatley eventually wrote a book of poetry. Before it could be published, she was examined by several prominent white men in Boston to determine if she, an enslaved black woman, was capable of writing the poems herself.

poems: few white Bostonians believed she could have written the poems by herself. The white male examiners concluded that Wheatley did indeed possess the intellectual acumen to write poetry, but even then, the book was first published in England.

Eventually, in 1773 her book of poetry, *Poems on Various Subjects, Religious and Moral* became the first book published by an African in America, but questions about her intellect and, by extension, that of other African Americans enslaved and free did not go away.

Thomas Jefferson, the most prominent arbiter of black people's intellectual ability, discredited Wheatley's poetry, saying that it did not change his belief that black people were inferior to whites. In his 1787 publication *Notes on the State of Virginia*, Jefferson wrote, "Misery is often the parent of the most affecting touches of poetry—among the blacks is misery enough, God knows, but no poetry. Love is the peculiar oestrum of the poet. Their love is ardent, but it kindles the senses only, not the imagination. Religion, indeed, has produced a Phyllis Whately [*sic*]; but it could not produce a poet. The compositions published under her name are below the dignity of criticism." In Jefferson's judgment Phillis Wheatley and others of African descent experienced emotions but lacked the capacity to translate them into the revered European poetic form.

Jefferson's disparaging remarks prompted a letter from Benjamin Banneker, a free black man from Maryland who worked on the initial survey of Washington, DC. Using his knowledge of astronomy, Banneker produced an almanac that he sent to Jefferson to convince him that a black person could indeed be intelligent. Banneker wrote that he knew that he was from a race considered to be intellectually inferior, but he hoped that Jefferson would be flexible enough to admit, when presented with evidence, that claims of black intellectual inferiority were untrue. He expected that Jefferson would "embrace every opportunity to eradicate that train of absurd and false ideas and opinions, which so generally prevails with respect to us." Jefferson responded, "No body wishes more than I do, to see such proofs as you exhibit, that nature has given to our black brethren talents equal to those of the other colors of men and that the appearance of the want of them, is owning merely to the degraded condition of their existence, both in Africa and America." Banneker was probably not pleased with this grudging response.

Jefferson and other whites had constructed a belief system that proclaimed black people their inferiors, then asserted that the alleged lack of intelligence actually rendered black people only suited for manual, mostly agricultural labor. They also contended that Africans' physical makeup, particularly their black skin, rendered them better able than whites to work in the heat of the South. This supposed dichotomy was articulated again and again; white people's minds were valuable while black people's value rested in their bodies.

Always subject to denigration and disparagement, enslaved people in the North and the South performed a wide array of labor, but from the 1600s to 1865 the vast majority worked in agriculture

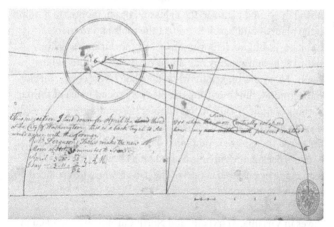

5. Benjamin Banneker, a free black man, created this diagram of the solar eclipse of April 3, 1791. He sent a copy of his almanac to Thomas Jefferson in an effort to convince him of African Americans' intelligence.

producing the cash crops that generated the wealth of the nation. The slave trade created mass consumer markets that traded sugarcane, sugar, rum, molasses, tobacco, indigo, coffee, rice, and cotton—all of which enslaved people produced. During the eighteenth and nineteenth centuries the number of people captured and sold into slavery expanded to meet the demands of planters, and once Congress abolished the Atlantic slave trade in America in 1808, a thriving domestic slave trade moved 1 million people from the Upper South to the Deep South and West for the express purpose of producing the crops that American and European economies demanded.

Tobacco, the first staple cash crop in the colonies, required a yearlong cycle of labor. In January and February enslaved people planted the seeds in the seedbeds. Workers covered the beds with leaves and pine needles to protect the seeds and young plants from predators and the cold weather; they prepared the fields into which the seedlings would be transplanted. In April they transplanted the leafed-out seedlings. After more growth, they moved the young plants to the fields and began months of tending to the plants—hilling soil to protect the roots and to enable drainage, re-hilling, removing worms, removing excess leaves to direct the sun's energy into about twelve leaves, and pulling weeds. This work took place while the plants were small and close to the ground, thus requiring that workers spend much of the day working bent over. During the summer the plants grew to a height of six to nine feet. When the leaves ripened in the fall, workers cut and cured them in well-ventilated dark, and dry tobacco barns. Workers packed the cured leaves into hogshead barrels that had been made by enslaved coopers. The barrels were then shipped north and to Europe.

Slaves in Virginia, Maryland, and North Carolina who worked in tobacco fields labored under a regimented gang system: overseers and drivers set the workers' pace and closely monitored their labor, using whipping and other forms of physical punishment to force people to work. Enslaved people rose early in the morning and worked until evening with breaks for meals. Owners usually provided monthly rations such as bacon, corn or cornmeal, potatoes, and sometimes molasses. On some plantations where the gang system was in use, owners required that enslaved people raise vegetables in assigned garden plots for their own consumption.

Enslaved people on tobacco and other plantations also received rations of clothing. It was commonplace for slaves to receive two outfits for the year, sometimes made from coarse Osnaburg cotton cloth imported from Germany, or woven from domestically grown hemp. For the winter, people might receive woolen clothing. Sometimes enslaved women received yards of cloth for making into clothing for their families. Children often went barefoot all year, while adults received rough leather ankle-high boots called brogans. On large plantations it was common for enslaved cobblers to fabricate these boots.

In South Carolina, rice emerged as the wealth-producing cash crop of the colony. Although agricultural labor was considered "unskilled labor," rice cultivation in South Carolina made clear the importance of possessing specific agricultural knowledge and skills. In the 1670s, when Englishmen who had settled in Barbados migrated to America to establish the colony of South Carolina, they brought enslaved Africans with them. The colonists made several attempts to develop saleable commodities for the international market, for example, slaves cultivated indigo, the plant used to produce blue dye, and some enslaved men worked as cowboys tending cattle. These same colonists also attempted to grow rice, but they did not know how. However, some of the enslaved people did have that knowledge, likely from their experience living on the grain coast of West Africa. Within a few years, the colony had its economic base, and the demand for slaves increased markedly. Ships' captains, eager to supply the demand advertised that they had "cargoes" of slaves from the grain coast who were skilled in rice cultivation. By 1705 rice had become the main source of the South Carolina colony's success.

Growing and processing rice required several steps. In South Carolina and Georgia, black men and women converted swamps and tidal marshes into rice fields; they and white planters engineered sophisticated irrigation systems with gates that they opened to flood the fields at the appropriate time in the growth of the crop. Further, they designed methods for ensuring that salt from brackish water did not make it onto the fields, and they built banks to protect against soil erosion.

Women constituted a majority of the labor force in the Low Country of South Carolina and in Georgia, and therefore did most of the work in rice cultivation: plowing, planting, weeding, hoeing, and harvesting in snake- and mosquito-infested environments. Women and girls sowed rice seeds sometimes using a heel-and-toe movement to dig the hole and cover it to protect the small grain, a practice that women in West Africa employed. When the seed germinated, the fields had to be hoed and weeded frequently. This was backbreaking work that enslaved people did with hand tools, standing in wet soil in hot, humid weather.

When the crop was ready in late August and early September, field hands chopped stalks of rice, stacked them on shallow boats, and transported them to the threshing yard. There, workers used a flailing stick, a pole with a stick attached to it, to beat the grain off the stalks without damaging the grain. They then winnowed the rice using handwoven fanner baskets to throw the rice into the air, relying on the breeze to blow away unwanted fragments of stalk and leaves. Then they polished the rice by pounding the hard shell away from the rice grain in wooden mortars and pestles made by enslaved people on the plantation. This process of polishing demanded both strength and skill—the pestle could weigh several pounds, and the workers had to be careful to remove the shell without cracking the rice grain, as this would reduce the price that

6. Although taken several decades after slavery ended, this photograph of women in Sapelo Island, Georgia, hulling rice with a mortar and pestle, demonstrates the method that enslaved women used on plantations in the 1700s and 1800s.

owners could receive for the product. Then they winnowed the grains again using the baskets.

Unlike tobacco in which people worked under a gang system, rice workers typically operated under a task system in which owners or overseers assigned each person a task for the day; when the task was done, the worker was free to stop working. Owners, overseers, and the enslaved men who worked as drivers meted out tasks based on age and physical ability. One planter described the amount of work that varied by the particular job that had to be done. "Each full hand [grown person] is required to turn or dig up one quarter of an acre of swamp land [rice land] per day," the planter noted. "In cutting ditches, the task is 600 feet—this number will be the length that each man will have to cut. In listing land each negro will do half an acre; in bedding land three-eighths of an acre; in trenching land for rice each man will trench three-quarters of an acre which will contain 180 rows; the women who sow will plant one and a half acres; in hoeing rice, corn, or potatoes, each negro will do one half acre if the land is in good order." Planters expected that each task would take a full day of labor.

In a system imported from Barbados, from which both colonists and slaves had come, enslaved people who worked under the task system also had to provide much of their own food, and this they did by cultivating the provision grounds that owners allotted them. When they finished working in the owner's rice fields, they turned to their own crops. Some people grew surplus crops that they then sold to their owners or in public marketplaces. On some plantations, enslaved people worked in the plantation's provision grounds raising crops such as potatoes, corn, and peas that would feed owners as well as slaves.

Each year, enslaved people produced tons of rice, which ships took to northern colonies and states, as well as to European countries including Spain, Portugal, the Netherlands, and England. Planters named the commodity "Carolina Gold" because of the color of the outer hull; indeed, the name was also appropriate because rice generated such wealth for them and the colony. In the 1750s, rice planters in South Carolina had the highest per capita income in the colonies.

By the 1790s, however, cotton outpaced all other crops. Cotton had been grown in small quantities in Virginia and the Carolinas since the early colonial period, but it was the American Revolution that began its precipitous increase. As some Americans boycotted English-made items including cloth and clothing, and as the war made importation more difficult, Americans turned to homegrown cotton to produce homespun textiles. The crop took off as a moneymaking commodity after 1793 with Eli Whitney's improved cotton gin. The gin was a simple device: a wooden box covered by a series of combs attached to a handle. As a worker cranked the handle, the combs separated seeds from the cotton fiber enabling the worker to clean ten times more cotton than extracting seeds by hand. Some planters installed these devices in gin houses on their own property, while others sent their cotton to be ginned in custom operations off the plantation. Either of these scenarios demanded the work of enslaved people as they operated the gins on their owner's plantation or hauled the cotton off the plantation to businesses where other enslaved people usually operated the gins.

The development of this new technology paralleled the growth of the British textile industry as the Industrial Revolution got under way. In the nineteenth century, enslaved people cultivated cotton in North Carolina, South Carolina, Georgia, Alabama, Mississippi, Tennessee, Arkansas, and Texas. Cotton became so profitable that in the 1790s some planters abandoned tobacco and indigo cultivation in favor of cotton crops.

Increased production of cotton and the improved ability to process it led to an increased demand for slave labor, and for the land on which to grow the crop. This was one motivator for westward expansion as the 1803 Louisiana Purchase by President

Thomas Jefferson made more lands available to Americans. In the 1830s, the forced removal of Cherokees, Choctaws, Chickasaws, Creeks, and Seminoles from the fertile lands of the southeastern United States, under the direction of President Andrew Jackson, amassed even more land for cotton cultivation and expansion of the wealth of white people. As Native Americans made the involuntary treks to what would become Indian Country or Oklahoma, white Americans dislocated approximately one million African Americans through the domestic slave trade, moving them from the Upper South to the Lower South and westward, destroying families, and severing community ties in order to create plantations and cultivate cotton.

Not all enslaved people lived in rural, agricultural areas; slavery also existed in urban spaces, where people worked in owner's homes and in commercial enterprises. The crops that enslaved workers produced required processing to ready them for the market, and very often, other slaves performed that labor as well. In the 1850s approximately 5 percent of enslaved people in the South performed industrial work. In factories in the urban areas of Richmond, Petersburg, Lynchburg, and Danville, Virginia, for example, enslaved men and women, most of them hired from their owners, worked in tobacco manufacturing factories in which they cleaned, dried, flavored, twisted, and lumped tobacco leaves into packages of chewing tobacco. In the 1840s and 1850s Richmond, the state capital, processed more tobacco than any other product (including flour and iron), and in 1860 Richmond ranked as the wealthiest southern industrial city.

Enslaved people also worked as spinners and weavers in the southern textile mills that operated in North Carolina, Georgia, Virginia, South Carolina, Alabama, and Mississippi in the antebellum period. Some mills used only enslaved people while some used a combination of slaves and free white people. These mills attempted to compete with northern and English mills that had been established earlier; some brought in experienced white workers from northern mills such as those in Lowell, Massachusetts, to supervise the local workers.

Once tobacco, rice, cotton, or other crops such as wheat, indigo, or sugarcane had been harvested or processed, they had to make their way to the market, whether in the South, the North, or in Europe. Here again, enslaved people did much of the work. They hauled products to the stations and ports, helped to load them onto ships and trains, and often worked on those same ships and trains. In fact, enslaved people helped to build the railroad lines on which the trains operated. Companies such as the Mississippi Railroad, the Georgia Railroad, and the Raleigh and Gaston Railroad in North Carolina owned the slaves; other companies hired them from owners.

The persistent theme here is that from the early 1700s until the Civil War, the labor of millions of African American slaves helped to produce the nation's economic growth. Their work varied by region and by the demands of the economy, but there was almost no limit to the range of labor they performed. A tally of the skills of runaway slaves in colonial South Carolina, identified forty-five different skills including carpenter, shoemaker, seamstress, butcher, "a kind of doctor," wagon driver, cattle hunter, silversmith, jeweler, boat pilot, and barber. Almost everything needed to run the enterprise was done or produced right on large plantations; enslaved people made barrels, shoes, clothing, iron work, farm tools, wagons, candles, quilts, bricks, and a long list of other products. Most slaves in the South lived on plantations and farms, and performed primarily agricultural tasks, but when the weather or the season made work in the fields impossible or unnecessary, they kept working. A Louisiana planter described his expectations for the people he owned on such days: "When the hands cannot work out[side], they must clean up the stables, mend and grease their gear, and sharpen and put in order their implements, clean up the quarters, pile the manure, etc.; the cribs, ox lots and stables require much work to keep them in good order, and when the weather is rainy or bad they can do this work, and I desire it to be particularly attended to."

Enslaved men and boys worked in incipient industries such as Thomas Jefferson's nail factory at his home plantation in Monticello, Virginia. At Boone Hall plantation in Charleston, South Carolina, enslaved people produced bricks that were used to construct buildings in downtown Charleston. In New Orleans, enslaved people crafted many of the elaborate metal railings that still surround porches and balconies in the French Quarter. On the Wessyngton Plantation near Nashville, Tennessee, enslaved people produced whisky, peach and apple brandy, and ham. At the Stagville Plantation in Durham, North Carolina, some of the nine hundred enslaved people made bricks, built their cabins, and constructed a massive wooden barn to house the mules bred on the plantation. Instead of using nails, the enslaved carpenters used the wooden peg-and-groove method popular in shipbuilding at the time.

Enslaved people worked in large-scale iron works in the South. They mined the iron ore and operated the furnaces that transformed the ore into pig iron. Much of this iron went into the building of railroads. Enslaved people also mined gold in North Carolina, Georgia, and Virginia, and later in California. They mined lead in Virginia and Missouri, and salt in Virginia, Kentucky, and Arkansas.

Slaves logged pine, cypress, and live oak; they worked in the sawmills that cut the trees into lumber. They distilled turpentine from pine trees in the Carolinas and Georgia. As they did in New Amsterdam, they built the infrastructure of southern colonies and states; they dug canals and levees and helped to build almost every southern railroad. They built ferries and ships, and sometimes operated the ferries. In the 1820s when steamboats became prevalent, slaves worked on board as deck hands, firemen, engineers, and pilots but were excluded from some positions that were reserved for white workers. When contractors designed and built bridges across rivers and streams, they used slave laborers, and one builder even used two enslaved architects. Even the federal government relied on slave labor; enslaved people supplied the bricks, lumber, and sandstone, and helped in the actual construction of the U.S. Capitol in Washington, DC. Enslaved people worked in federal navy yards, arsenals, and fortifications until the late 1850s.

Saying that enslaved *people* performed the work is no mere generality; although some industries used mostly male slaves, many also used women and children to carry out the tasks. Women, and sometimes children, worked in textile, hemp, and tobacco factories. They worked in sugar refining and rice milling. Half of the workers who dug South Carolina's Santee Canal were women, and women helped to build the Louisiana levees. Enslaved women worked in lumbering and in coal and iron mining. They worked in iron works, with furnaces and forges. By the mid-nineteenth century, many elite whites divided white men and women into separate spheres, but for enslaved people, only porous boundaries existed between male and female labor. Still, some jobs, particularly in the trades, remained the realm of enslaved men, such as blacksmithing, a profession that could provide some advantages as such artisans were more likely to be hired out by owners.

This practice of hiring slaves occurred frequently in both the North and South in the colonial as well as the antebellum period. Owners hired out people who performed a wide range of labor. One source estimates that in 1860 half the people who worked in Virginia tobacco factories were hired slaves. An owner could do quite well by collecting payment for the services of someone he or she owned. In most cases the owner collected a fee directly from the person who hired the slaves, and the person hiring also fed and clothed the slave for the year of the agreement. Less frequently, the enslaved person, usually a male artisan with marketable skills, was allowed to hire out himself. This meant that he could find a job, perhaps many miles away from an owner, negotiate a price, pay an agreed-upon portion to his owner, and use the rest for housing, food, and other needs. This arrangement provided the possibility that this enslaved person could save and thereby eventually purchase his freedom.

However, having slaves hire themselves out raised objections from white residents in some jurisdictions who feared that having slaves "going about as if free" presented a threat to the stability of the institution. These were not isolated concerns, and it was often illegal under state law to allow a slave to hire his or her time. In Edenton, North Carolina, for example, grand juries indicted enslaved people for "living to themselves in the town of Edenton, and hiring their own time," or for "keeping house and enjoying all the privileges" of a free person. The grand jury indicted an owner because he allowed his slave Sylva "to keep house to her self as a freewoman." Further, the owner "did permit his said slave Sylva to go at large as a free woman exercising her own discretion in the employment of her own time." It was too complicated if enslaved people, rather than being directed, overseen, and subjected to physical punishments, could freely move about and earn their own money. Hired out slaves might begin to think that they were free and some whites might begin to treat them as though they were free. They often lived and worked in urban areas away from their owners, with a mobility that was anathema to enslavement. Whites feared that any degree of freedom could pose a threat to the stability of slavery. Some enslaved people wanted to hire themselves out for precisely that reason.

It may seem paradoxical, but many enslaved people took great pride in their work even though they were owned and worked for no compensation. Valuing their skills and taking pride in the work meant that their labor was not wasted; it sustained their egos and their need to have meaningful lives. Cognizant of their own hard and meticulous labor as well as the country's reliance upon it, many enslaved people developed a sense that this was as much their country as anyone else's—they had built it.

Chapter 4
Struggles for control

It took persistent effort on the part of slave owners and their allies to keep slavery in place, to make people work without pay, and to sustain the arguments that justified the forced labor of other human beings. It required such great effort because enslaved people did not always simply submit to the demands of their owners; many struggled in ways large and small against owners' plans, orders, and attempts to dominate them. Not every enslaved person resisted, and no one resisted all the time, but from the start—from the slave ships crossing the Atlantic to the beginnings of slavery in Virginia, New York, and Massachusetts—Africans and African Americans fought against those who endeavored to control every aspect of their lives. White elites deployed a vast range of mechanisms to gain and maintain control over enslaved people, including, violence, legislation, slave patrols, religion, paternalistic demeaning behavior, and racist proslavery ideology. And enslaved people drew from a reservoir of strategies that included literacy, religion, escape, malingering, and rebellion, to resist enslavement and its attendant hardships.

Slave owners clearly held much more power than enslaved people, but even the most oppressed were never completely powerless: they could assert their objections by withholding their labor by pretending to be sick, or by breaking the tools necessary for carrying out the owner's tasks. Despite the grave imbalance of power, slavery was to some degree a negotiated relationship, and slave owners and others with political power had to constantly shift and reinforce their strategies to counter the actions of the enslaved among them. Slaves most often dared not express their objections to being enslaved or refuse to obey any particular command, yet enough of them resisted to produce a relentless struggle between the dominant and the subordinate.

The words of two men from North Carolina, written in 1829, elucidate the tensions that existed between owners and slaves, between blacks and whites, and between domination and resistance. In an opinion, which upheld the actions of a white man who shot the enslaved woman whom he had hired, the chief justice of the North Carolina Supreme Court Thomas Ruffin wrote: "The power of the master must be absolute to render the submission of the slave perfect." In contrast, David Walker, a free black man, declared in a pamphlet, "The whites want slaves, and want us for their slaves, but some of them will curse the day they ever saw us. As true as the sun ever shone in its meridian splendor, my colour will root some of them out of the very face of the earth. They shall have enough of making slaves of, and butchering, and murdering us in the manner which they have." Ruffin expressed a belief that an owner or his agent had the right to exert absolute power over a slave, and that with the infliction of enough violence enslaved people could in fact be subdued. Walker, on the other hand, conceded that violence had indeed forced people to submit, but he was certain that such power could neither be absolute nor enduring. In his view, slave owners would have to recompense for their brutality. The social positions and the rhetoric of these two men could not have been any more at odds, nor could their beliefs about the legitimacy of slavery. Still, they agreed that violence underpinned the power of slave owners. Unlike Ruffin, though, Walker predicted that violence on the part of black people was necessary to undermine and ultimately destroy whites' power.

WALKER'S

APPEAL,

With a Brief Sketch of his Life.

BY

HENRY HIGHLAND GARNET.

AND ALSO

GARNET'S ADDRESS

TO THE SLAVES OF THE UNITED STATES OF AMERICA.

NEW-YORK:
Printed by J. H. Tobitt, 9 Spruce-st.
1848.

7. David Walker wrote this *Appeal* in which he denounced slave holders as violating the strictures of the Bible, and challenged enslaved and free African Americans to rise up against slavery. Some southern states responded by imposing harsher restrictions on African American mobility and literacy.

Thomas Ruffin and David Walker occupied starkly different spheres within antebellum America. Ruffin, a wealthy white man, wrote his opinion about power and submission from the lofty perch of the judicial bench in the case of *State v. Mann*. In that case, Lydia, a woman owned by a minor child named Elizabeth Jones, was hired out to John Mann by Elizabeth's guardian. Mann had financial problems and was likely unable to purchase slaves of his own, so he hired Lydia for one year. Mann testified at his trial that he had become tired of Lydia's insolence, and when he attempted to punish her, she ran, and he shot her. Lydia continued running and made it back to the home of Elizabeth's guardian, who convinced the state's attorney to charge Mann with assaulting Elizabeth's property. A grand jury in Chowan County, North Carolina, indicted Mann, and a jury of twelve white men convicted him of assault and battery upon Lydia.

In the state supreme court, however, Justice Ruffin, himself a slave owner who was deeply entrenched in the political, social, and economic life of the state, found differently. He overruled the jury's decision, finding instead that owners and their agents had the absolute right to control slaves. Although he claimed to think that slavery was an abomination and looked forward to its demise, Ruffin nonetheless took this opportunity to uphold the violence that was essential to keeping slavery in place. The aim of slavery, he reasoned, "is the profit of the master, his security and the public safety." A slave, in contrast, was doomed forever to "live without knowledge and without the capacity to make anything his own, and to toil that another may reap the fruits." The slave, he said, could not be expected to submit voluntarily to doing this unpaid labor, rather, "such obedience is the consequence only of uncontrolled authority over the body." This violently enforced obedience, Ruffin argued, was an inherent element of slavery, because for the slave to remain a slave, the owner must have full dominion.

David Walker, in contrast, although free, was by no means wealthy. He was born in Wilmington, North Carolina, and inherited the free status of his mother, despite the fact that his father was enslaved. He made his way to Boston, where he operated a store that sold used clothing. Nonetheless, Walker considered himself threatened by slavery, and he urged other free black people to challenge the institution because in a country that practiced racial slavery, every free black person's liberty was vulnerable. In his *Appeal to the Coloured Citizens of the World, but in particular, and very expressly, to those of the United States of America,* Walker vehemently denounced slavery and slave owners, and he beseeched both free and enslaved African Americans to rise up against their oppressors.

Literacy enabled these two men with opposing values and stakes in slavery to advance their ideas, but while white southerners received Ruffin's ability to write as legitimate, they perceived Walker's as the threat he intended it to be. Not only were Walker's incendiary words deemed dangerous, whites in the South viewed literacy among black people and particularly enslaved people as threatening and frightening. The ability to read was deemed dangerous in a society in which slavery relied on domination by whites and subordination of blacks. Walker reflected on this fear on the part of whites when he claimed, "for coloured people to acquire learning in this county, makes tyrants quake and tremble on their sandy foundation. Why, what is the matter? Why, they know that their infernal deeds of cruelty will be make known to the world.... The bare name of educating the coloured people scares our cruel oppressors almost to death." Not only could literacy expose the cruelty of slavery to the world, but having literate black people would render it more difficult to sustain the Jeffersonian claims of black intellectual inferiority. Literacy, then, was one of the many grounds on which owners and slaves contended.

This tension became palpable in legislation that most southern slave states enacted to prohibit teaching enslaved people, and in some instances, any person of color, to read or write. The South

Carolina colony was the first to inscribe the fear of black literacy into legislation. In 1740, prompted by the growth of the black population in the colony as well as the Stono Rebellion in 1739, the Negro Act outlawed teaching slaves to read or write because literacy would bring "great inconveniences." The antiliteracy provision was part of a larger "Act for the Better Ordering of Negroes and Other Slaves," which regulated behavior and prescribed punishments. In 1800, the state enacted new legislation that stated, "Whereas the law heretofore enacted for the government of slaves, free Negroes, mulattoes, and mestizos, have been found insufficient for the keeping them in due subordination," and imposed new prohibitions and punishments for anyone who taught slaves to read or write and for the enslaved students themselves.

In 1834 the South Carolina legislature again saw the need to ban literacy among enslaved people and free people of color. Legislatures in several other colonies and states passed similar laws, and as South Carolina did, they connected literacy to unrest and declared that keeping black people subservient to whites was necessary to prevent uprisings. The North Carolina legislation, for example, said that teaching slaves to read and write "has a tendency to excite dissatisfaction in their minds, and to produce insurrection and rebellion, to the manifest injury of the citizens of the State." These laws sought to prevent black literacy and they used the threat of imprisonment and state sanctioned violence to force adherence. Legislatures authorized legions of law enforcement officers including magistrates, sheriffs, constables, militia officers, and officers of the slave patrols to break down doors, imprison, whip, and or fine black people who were caught learning to read or write, as well as anyone who taught them.

David Walker's *Appeal* prompted more legislation. The prospect of thousands of enslaved people reading or listening to Walker's injunction to rise up is exactly what terrified owners and other whites. In December 1829, just months after it was published, the

The Georgia anti-literacy law, 1829

An Act to be entitled an act, to amend the several laws now in force in this State, regulating quarantine in the several sea ports of this State, and to prevent the circulation of written or printed papers within this State calculated to excite disaffection among the coloured people of this state, and to prevent said people from being taught to read or write.

Section 10. *And it be further enacted*, That if any slave, negro, mustizzo, [*sic*] or free person of colour, or any other person, shall circulate, bring or cause to be circulated or brought into this state or aid or assist in any manner, or be instrumental in aiding or assisting in the circulation or bringing into this state, or in any manner concerned in any printed or written pamphlet, paper or circular, for the purposes for exciting to insurrection, conspiracy or resistance among the slaves, negroes, or free persons of colour, of this state against their owners or the citizens of this state, the said person or persons offending against this section of this act, shall be punished with death.

Section 11—*And be it further enacted*, that if any slave, negro, or free person of colour or any white person shall teach any other slave, negro, or free person of colour, to read or write either written or printed characters, the said free person of color, or slave, shall be punished by fine and whipping, or fine or shipping at the discretion of the court; and if a white person so offending, he, she or they shall be punished with fine, not exceeding five hundred dollars, and imprisonment, in the common jail at the discretion of the court before whom said offender is tried.

Appeal made its way to Savannah, Georgia, smuggled there on a ship by black sailors. The Georgia legislature quickly crafted a response that outlawed teaching "any slave, negro, or free person of colour" to read. It also punished any black or other person who brought "any printed or written pamphlet, paper or circular, for the purposes of exciting to insurrection, conspiracy or resistance among the slaves, negroes or free persons of color" into the state. One month later, Louisiana banned any publication that, like Walker's *Appeal,* had a "tendency to produce discontent among the free coloured population of the state, or insubordination among the slaves," and punished the writer or distributor with either death or imprisonment at hard labor for life. The statute also punished any public discourse against slavery, prohibited teaching slaves to read or write, and provided imprisonment for up to one year for anyone caught teaching them. In August, David Walker died suddenly in his home in Boston. Whites from the South had offered a monetary reward for his death, and even more for delivering him to the South alive, but there was no conclusive evidence that he had been murdered.

Despite legal prohibitions and threats of severe punishment, many African Americans placed a high value on literacy and, just as their owners did, some made linkages between literacy and freedom, and literacy and power. Although the majority of enslaved people never learned to read and write, many took great risks to become literate. They wanted access to information, and they wanted to be able to communicate with family members who were sold away from them. In a regime that required any black person to have written permission from an owner, or in the case of free people, a white guardian, to move about, some wanted to be able to forge their passes. Many wanted to be able to read the Bible for themselves in order to have direct access to the lessons contained in the scripture. Some wanted proof of what they suspected: that the minister whom the slave owner provided for them really could find other passages on a Sunday than the often repeated, "Servants obey your master."

Given the laws and regulations, many former slaves spoke of having to "steal" an education, and they employed a range of strategies to become literate. Some learned the rudiments of reading from an owner's wife who believed that everyone should be able to read the Bible. Frederick Douglass's slave mistress had this goal in mind when she began to teach him to read as a young boy, but his owner soon intervened, proclaiming that being literate would spoil him for slavery. Some people taught themselves by using Noah Webster's *Blue Back Speller*, which offered basic reading lessons. Enslaved men and boys often got help in this endeavor by asking, challenging, or bribing white men or boys whom they encountered while doing errands for their owners. Women who worked in the owner's house sometimes surreptitiously received help with spelling from the children in their care. Men spoke of hiding the speller under their hats; women hid it in their bosoms awaiting an opportune moment for a lesson from the white children in their care. Those who gained rudimentary literacy skills taught others to read and write, sometimes in their cabins, or out in the woods at night, or on Sundays when owners left the plantation to attend church or to visit socially. In more urban areas such as Hampton and Norfolk, Virginia, and Savannah, Georgia, enslaved children attended secret, illegal schools held in the black teacher's home.

As owners feared, enslaved people's literacy undermined owner's authority. In Baltimore, while hired out to work on the docks, Frederick Douglass read a newspaper and learned for the first time of an abolitionist movement in the North, which aimed to destroy slavery. Douglass thus used his literacy to expand his knowledge of a world beyond his owner's control. He also used his skills to forge a pass in which he pretended to be his owner. By writing that pass, Douglass was able to break away from the physical bonds of his owner. Learning about the existence of the abolition movement also helped him to develop a belief that freedom was possible.

Some literate slaves used the ability to read the Bible to challenge the dominant white ideology that black people were inferior and suited only to be slaves. Indeed, Christianity proved to be both a method for enforcing subordination as well as a means for challenging oppression as slave owners and enslaved people alike interpreted the Bible to suit their conflicting desires and purposes. Even after colonial laws made it clear that slaves' acceptance of Christianity would not free them, many slave owners refrained from encouraging Christianity among enslaved people. They feared the implications of the New Testament teaching that all humans are equal in the sight of God. In response, some ministers promised that Christianity would render Africans and African Americans better slaves because they would be taught to serve their earthly masters out of a sense of Christian duty and to live in fear of judgment in the next life.

Perhaps not surprisingly, for the first one hundred years in the American colonies, most Africans and their descendants did not embrace Christianity. Their owners did not encourage or force it; it did not free them but in fact aimed to make them more submissive, and its rituals were unfamiliar. Instead, they held on to their own rites and practices that included drumming, dancing, spirit possession, and sometimes animal sacrifice—activities Europeans considered heathen.

This resistance to Christianity began to change with the religious revivals of the First Great Awakening in the 1740s, when such evangelical preachers as Jonathan Edwards and George Whitefield preached messages of salvation and immediate conversion. In addition to white men, many black people, white women, and Native Americans attended and participated in large outdoor revivals and camp meetings at which some professed salvation and even became exhorters, taking on the role of preachers. Enslaved people understood the messages of the evangelists and could claim a connection to Christ, therefore according to doctrine, rendering them equal to whites.

The evangelical form of worship attracted African Americans and Africans who appreciated its expressive nature, its clear and direct path to Christ, and its promise of equality under God. Still, although some enslaved people became evangelists, sometimes even proselytizing to white people, this sense of a broadening sphere did not result in their physical freedom. Indeed, as more slaves accepted Christianity, owners moved to restrict gatherings of slaves and other black people for religious services, and some tried to use Christianity to subdue enslaved people, preaching messages of submission and obedience.

To regulate the messages that enslaved people drew from the Bible, some states prohibited gatherings of blacks—without a white man present—for church services. But when these laws or the rules of owners attempted to control the messages of black religious worship, enslaved people held secret services and meetings. People met in the woods at night or in cabins far from the owner's house, and worshipped in ways they saw fit.

Enslaved people not only found ways to worship out of the sight and hearing of whites, they also adapted Christianity to meet their own needs and interpreted lessons from the Old Testament to apply to their lives in bondage. In the book of Exodus, God sent Moses to lead the children of Israel out of bondage in Egypt, and some enslaved African Americans shaped the story to mean that God would send a Moses to liberate *them* from slavery in America. They preached these stories to one another and shaped the promises into songs that they sang while at work and during worship. Songs with lyrics such as "Go Down, Moses, way down in Egypt's land; Tell old Pharaoh, to let my people go," reaffirmed for them the belief that they would not always be slaves.

Some whites, of course, interpreted the Bible very differently. They contended that both the Old and New Testaments supported slavery. Some claimed, for example, that according to the book of Genesis, Africans and their descendants were intended to be slaves. Africans, they said, were descended from Ham, who had looked upon his drunk and naked father, Noah, without turning away. Noah cursed Ham's son Canaan and his descendants, saying, "servants of servants shall they be to their brethren." Canaan, this interpretation reasoned, was black and lived in Africa: therefore all Africans were condemned to be slaves forever. From the New Testament, theologians who supported slavery took the words of Paul to support their enslavement of people and to demand obedience and subservience from them. They preached these lessons over and over. From Colossians: "Servants, obey in all things your masters according to the flesh; not with eyeservice, as menpleasers; but in singleness of heart, fearing God." And from Ephesians: "Servants, be obedient to them that are *your* masters according to the flesh, with fear and trembling, in singleness of your heart, as unto Christ." The message to enslaved people was that God approved of their enslavement and that they should work faithfully for their owners, even when the owner was not watching, because God would see and judge them.

Although some slaves thought that it must have been a part of God's plan that they should suffer in slavery for a time, many enslaved people and former slaves tired of hearing these lessons about obedience and subservience. They complained that the white ministers seemed unable to find any other messages in the Bible, and understood that these lessons were intended to uphold the power of their owners. Other African Americans believed that God would judge whites harshly for having enslaved them. Some thought that the avowed Christianity of slave owners and those who supported slavery was inauthentic and corrupt, and that it misused and misrepresented the Bible. Frederick Douglass and Harriet Jacobs, both former slaves, claimed that some of the worst slave owners called themselves Christians. Douglass wrote, "I love the pure, peaceable, and impartial Christianity of Christ: I therefore hate the corrupt, slaveholding, women-whipping, cradle-plundering, partial and hypocritical Christianity of the land. Indeed, I can see no reason, but the most deceitful one, for calling the religion of this land Christianity. I look upon it as the climax of all misnomers, the boldest of all frauds, and the grossest of all libels. I am filled with unutterable loathing when I contemplate the religious pomp and show, together with the horrible inconsistencies, which every where surround me." And David Walker asked, "Is not God a God of justice to all his creatures? [I]f he gives peace and tranquility to tyrants, and permits them to keep our fathers, our mothers, ourselves and our children in eternal ignorance and wretchedness, to support them and their families, would he be to us a God of justice?" Walker's questions suggested that because God *is* a God of justice, it was not possible that he would condone the mistreatment of one group of his "creatures."

Efforts to regulate and control slaves emanated from legislatures, ministers, and of course from individual owners who had a great deal of discretion to keep their slaves in "due subordination." One planter in Georgia recommended that every plantation should have a code of laws, written or unwritten, to regulate slaves and to make clear to them that "the master will sit in righteous judgment and visit with just and certain punishment all transgressions." The "master" in this owner's words, sounded a great deal like the God of the Bible.

Owners employed a mixture of violence and paternalism to keep the people they owned in their places of servility. Even as they exercised control, they also wanted to be perceived by both their slaves and outsiders as firm and caring masters with dominion over their slaves. Some planters paternalistically spoke of the people they owned as part of their large outside family, in contrast to their inside family that consisted of a wife and children. They said that they fed, clothed, and protected their slaves, and in return the slaves labored for them. In this schema, there should have been no need for violence, but despite some whites' claims that enslaved people were servile by nature and perfectly suited to be slaves, and despite assertions that owners took good care of their slaves, most planters agreed with Justice Ruffin that violence was a necessary measure to extract labor and obedience from enslaved people.

Planters who could afford to employ help often distanced themselves from physical violence by delegating punishment to overseers or to jailers who punished other people's slaves for a living. These owners sought to make a fine distinction between "correction" and "punishment," sometimes urging their employees and delegates to administer whippings only for correction and prevention. They urged overseers not to administer punishment out of anger or with passion, as this would lead slaves to run away. Additionally, they thought that passion revealed a lack of control and that mastery demanded self-control. Owners also warned that punishment should not leave scars. Although expressed as emanating from a sense of concern about the slaves, this view was also in the owner's self-interest: scars signaled to potential purchasers that this slave might be a troublemaker, therefore reducing his or her value in the market.

To avoid administering whippings, or when corporal punishment was not effective, owners employed a vast array of "corrections" and "punishments." They locked people up at night; they denied passes to leave the plantation, a particularly painful punishment for men whose wives and children lived on other plantations. Despite all of their power, owners and overseers knew that their punishments might meet with resistance; "a violent and passionate threat," one owner cautioned, "will often scare the best disposed negro to the woods." Running to the woods was an undesirable consequence because this action deprived owners of the enslaved person's labor. Timed well, the absence of even one slave could have serious consequences for an owner's finances.

For some slaves, absconding from a plantation temporarily was not enough, nor was negotiating or resisting the wishes and demands of owners. Raising intellectual challenges to their domination and subjugation was not enough. Breaking tools that could be repaired was not enough. While some believed that God would have vengeance, others thought vengeance was theirs and took matters into their own hands. Owners gave themselves the right to use physical violence to discipline and control slaves, but some slaves challenged this right and asserted their own right to self-defense and to autonomy. These enslaved people, who were always in the minority among enslaved populations, returned violence for violence or struck preemptively; violence existed on a spectrum ranging from fighting back or resisting punishment to premeditated murder or arson to outright rebellion. When Frederick Douglass's owner hired him out to a Mr. Covey, whose task was to break his rebellious spirit, Douglass refused one day to submit to any more whippings and fought back, successfully subduing Covey. When Ellen Turner's owner attempted to punish her for hanging an image of Abraham Lincoln on her bedroom wall, Turner refused to be whipped and fought back. In daring to physically challenge the authority of these white men, Douglass and Turner risked being whipped even more harshly, being sold, or killed.

Some people rose up and took action in efforts to escape from slavery or to bring slavery to an end. The first revolts took place on the ships that brought Africans to the New World, and uprisings, large and small, occurred over time in the colonies and states. In New York on a Sunday morning in April 1712, a group of enslaved men and two enslaved women set fire to the outhouse of the owner of two of them. Historians suggest that many who participated in the rebellion had recently arrived in the colony and found the constrictions and limitations to be much more severe than the sort of slavery with which they were familiar in their communities in Africa, where there was more room for movement out of slavery and the possibility of gaining some freedoms even while enslaved. Now under English rule, and well beyond the charter generation of slavery, New York did not offer any of the limited flexibility that the first eleven slaves in Dutch New Amsterdam had been able to negotiate. After setting the fire, the slaves killed nine and wounded seven of the white residents who responded to put out the fire. As they faced capture, six of the rebels committed suicide. Colonial authorities arrested as many as seventy blacks, convicted twenty-six, and executed twenty-one. As frequently occurred following uprisings, the legislature put even more restrictive rules in place to control enslaved as well as free black people in the colony; the law imposed stricter curfews for slaves; it became more difficult for owners to manumit slaves; and any slave freed after 1712 could not own real estate. Finally, the law had the potential effect of not only restricting blacks but also elevating whites, as any white person could arrest any slave who violated the curfew rules and whip him or her.

In South Carolina, where by 1710 there were more enslaved Africans and African Americans than whites, owners lived with anxiety and fear of insurrection. This only worsened when in 1733 enslaved people received encouragement from the Spanish colony of Florida through an edict that promised freedom to any slave who made it to the garrison at St. Augustine, Florida. At first those who escaped were disappointed when the Spanish themselves enslaved them, but in 1738 the colony began to live up to its word, freed the former runaways, and established a settlement for them north of St. Augustine in the Pueblo de Gracia Real de Santa Terese de Mose, also known as Fort Mose or Moosa. This settlement became a sanctuary and intended destination for enslaved people in South Carolina. The Spanish and English governments were at odds, and Spain hoped to gain help to defend against and attack the English colonies.

On September 9, 1739, a group of twenty slaves gathered early in the morning near the Stono River about twenty miles from Charleston. It was a Sunday, the one day of the week on which most enslaved people were not expected to work. Led by an enslaved man named Jemmy, the group broke into a store that sold firearms and gunpowder, killed the storekeepers, and left their heads on the front steps. Now armed, they robbed a house, killing the owner and his two children. The group was clearly interested in revenge as well as escape. They headed to a tavern where they spared the life of the tavern keeper because he was known to be a good man and kind to his slaves. The group attacked several other homes, killing whites. In at least one instance, slaves hid their owners and were later rewarded for their loyalty. As the group moved, they added more enslaved people, some forcibly so as to reduce the chances of betrayal, some voluntarily.

At about 11:00 o'clock, the lieutenant governor and four other men happened to be riding in the direction of the rebels. Realizing the situation they turned, rode away, and sounded the alarm. Within hours, a militia company consisting of planters, arrived on horseback at the open field where the rebels had stopped to drum and dance, evidently in hopes of calling other slaves to join them. The two groups exchanged fire, but in the end the white men proved to be far more heavily armed and skilled, and won this skirmish. The planters decapitated the slaves and placed their heads on mileposts in the area. Some of the slaves escaped in small groups with plans to carry on or to return to their plantations. The militia, joined by a few Native Americans who became paid slave catchers, searched the area. It took one week for all the slaves to be caught and killed. In all, twenty-one whites and forty-four slaves were killed during the revolt. The rebellion was put down, but white planters continued to be fearful; in South Carolina there were more black people than whites, giving rise to widespread fears of insurrection. Some of the white families moved away, and the government of the colony paid rewards to blacks and Indians who had acted against the rebellion. It also created a special patrol along the Stono River. Slave owners feared that the very people who made them rich could also be their enemies and not only deprive them of labor, but worse still, kill them. In June 1740 lawmakers learned from an enslaved man of an impending rebellion among about 150 slaves to capture arms from a store and attack Charleston. Fifty slaves were caught and hanged for this conspiracy.

Owners could not rest. In May 1740 the South Carolina legislature enacted a new Negro Act, a much more restrictive slave code that outlawed teaching slaves to read and write, and severely restricted black mobility. In addition, slaves were no longer allowed to grow their own food or earn their own money. Slave owners all over the South now faced a dilemma: in the 1740s rice, indigo, tobacco, and cotton were wealth-producing cash crops that required an extensive work force. Plantation owners needed to remain alert and implement ever-new methods to keep enslaved people not only producing crops but "in their place" to prevent further rebellions.

Plots and rumors of conspiracy surfaced from time to time, but the largest and most deadly rebellion took place in Virginia on August 22, 1831, when a literate preacher named Nat Turner led between sixty and eighty enslaved people in an uprising that shook the entire country. Turner considered himself a Christian and said he received visions from God about the timing of the revolt. Although early missionaries had argued that Christianity would render slaves docile and concerned only with performing their duties to their earthly masters, the leaders of some of these rebellions were indeed religious men and may have acquired leadership roles in the rebellions precisely because of their roles as religious leaders.

Turner and his fellow rebels planned to kill all white people in their path and capture Jerusalem, the county seat of Southampton County, Virginia. Turner, along with fellow slaves Sam, Nelson, Hark, Henry, Will, Nelson, and Jack, all of whom had planned the revolt, set out before dawn and went from house to house killing white men, women, and children. Turner himself belonged to a nine-year-old child, which may have helped him to justify killing even very young children. The group of rebels grew throughout the morning and by midday they had killed fifty-five people in eleven homes. Soon however, local militias as well as ones from North Carolina responded, and captured or killed all the rebels, except Turner who eluded capture for two months. Once caught, he too was executed.

The terror of the rebellion provoked fear among whites in Virginia. Thomas Dew, professor at the College of William and Mary, wrote that even after the rebellion had been put down, the participants had been executed, and many whites had concluded that Nat Turner was a fanatic, "still the excitement remained, still the repose of the commonwealth was disturbed, for the ghastly horrors of the Southampton tragedy could not immediately be banished from the mind." Again, whites could not rest.

The legislature debated the idea of ending slavery in Virginia altogether. Members of the House of Delegates argued that having free blacks in the state would encourage slaves to revolt; thus all free black people should be removed from the state and sent to Africa. Some argued that their own wealth and the wealth of the state was tied to slavery, but others countered that it was simply too dangerous to keep slaves in their midst. Henry Berry, himself a slave owner, argued that there could be no rest until all the slaves were free. The legislature, he said, had already done all it could to keep slaves submissive, but it was not working. "Sir," he argued, "we have, as far as possible closed every avenue by which light might enter their mind; we have only to go one step further—to extinguish the capacity to see the light, and our work would be completed; they would then be reduced to the level of the beasts of the field, and we should be safe; and I am not certain that we would not do it, if we could find out the necessary process—and that under the plea of necessity." Berry believed that it was a mistake to think that whites could ever completely subdue blacks. Could slaves live among those who were free and not know what freedom is? If they thought they had the power to assert their freedom, wouldn't they? Berry thought they certainly would, and he predicted, "a death struggle must come between the two classes, in which one or the other will be extinguished forever. Like a mighty avalanche," he said, "it is rolling towards us, accumulating weight and impetus at every turn. And, sir, if we do nothing to arrest its progress, it will ultimately overwhelm and destroy us forever." To avoid what he saw as an imminent calamity,

Berry advocated a plan of gradual emancipation in which owners could hold on to their slaves for the present, but the institution would eventually die away.

Nonetheless, a majority of legislators concluded that the economic and social structure of the state would collapse without slavery. As Dew later argued, "It is in truth the slave labour in Virginia which gives value to her soil and her habitations—take away this and you pull down the atlas that upholds the whole system—eject from the state the whole slave population, and we risk nothing in the prediction, that on the day in which it shall be accomplished, the worn soils of Virginia will not bear the paltry price of the government lands in the West, and the Old Dominion will be a 'waste howling wilderness,'—'the grass shall be seen growing in the streets, and the foxes peeping from their holes.'" The legislature upheld slavery with even stronger and more oppressive laws that constricted the behavior of enslaved people. In March 1832 the Virginia House of Delegates restricted preaching by black people as their interpretations of the scriptures were seen as disruptive to the peace of white society. Nat Turner had, after all, been a preacher.

Many whites lived in fear of organized violence by slaves, and Henry Berry predicted that the force of black people's opposition to their oppression would eventually destroy Virginia. Unlike their counterparts in Jamaica or Brazil where there were more frequent and larger uprisings, African Americans lived surrounded by white people and white power in the form of weapons, overseers, drivers, slave patrols, militia, local law enforcement officers, and, after the 1780s, the federal military power of the United States. Where could they go? The slaves who had participated in the Stono Rebellion were heading to Florida to live under the protection of a separate sovereign power. Nat Turner himself had plans to get to Jerusalem, the Southampton County seat, but what would he and the others have done there? They certainly could not have simply declared their freedom or ordered an end to slavery. Although blacks constituted 60 percent of the county's population, whites owned the guns, and they held the power to put down the insurrection.

Turner's was the sort of violent uprising David Walker had urged two years earlier in his *Appeal*. Walker had also condemned African Americans for complacently accepting their condition as slaves or free people in northern states without equal rights or opportunities. But he failed to articulate the consequences for those who rebelled or attempted to escape. Indeed, considering the seeming futility of the revolt, some people then, as now, concluded that Turner must have been insane to raise a violent challenge to such a ubiquitous and seemingly invulnerable institution. Individual slaves could and did escape to northern states once slavery ended there, but even in those states they had to hide their status of runaway slave because the U.S. Constitution subjected them to being returned to owners. Many people felt they were trapped in slavery. Some became accustomed to it and perhaps believed it was their lot in life. Some likely never questioned the racial hierarchy, economic inequities, and distorted power relationships into which they were born. Others contemplated a way out.

As Henry Berry saw it, whites in Virginia made every effort to repress African Americans. If slave owners could somehow find a way to render enslaved people inhuman enough not to contrive plots to free themselves and to harm whites, yet human enough to be able to do the thinking required to complete their jobs, whites could be both rich *and* safe. For whites, the challenge was how to protect the institution of slavery: to have people who produced wealth and were satisfied with living in dire poverty; to have people who would submit to "correction" without challenging owners' power and authority; and to continue the repression and submission of an entire race of people. For African Americans, the challenge was how to assert their humanity and undermine whites' power without sacrificing their lives. The challenges for both slave owners and slaves continued as long as slavery did.

Chapter 5
Surviving slavery

People may not have survived the hard labor and the violence, the domination and the degradation of slavery, had they not found ways of nurturing their spirits. Though they wept, they also sometimes laughed. Sometimes when they worked, they also sang, and to make the day go faster or to break up the monotony, some syncopated their work rhythms. They formed families even though legal marriage was denied them, and they had children. And when slave owners destroyed those families through sale, some people continued to love the ones whom they had lost, even as they formed new families. Most enslaved people did not escape or engage in active rebellion; instead, they focused on living their lives, resisting when they could, exerting individual agency when possible. This agency could take the form of calling a child by the name the parents chose, rather than that imposed by an owner; hunting and fishing to supplement and vary a diet of owner-issued rations; learning to read and write. People shaped their circumscribed circumstances into lives that included not only pain and suffering but also pleasure, hope, and love.

In order to survive both physically and psychically, African captives first had to figure out how to communicate with their captors, with ships' mates, plantation owners, and other captives. They often strained to decipher other African languages and dialects, and they needed to read facial expressions and body language to unravel what Europeans wanted of them. Language adaptations began on the way to the African coast as captives passed from one community to another, sometimes spending weeks or months enslaved within Africa. Locally dialects were similar, but the farther one traveled from home, the more likely that he would be exposed to and might have to learn new ways of speaking. Then there was the shock of the coast, where African captives encountered, usually for the first time, Europeans who spoke in completely incomprehensible words and tones.

Once in America, the confusion and adaptations continued. It is difficult now to imagine how Africans and their descendants in America sounded from the early 1600s to the 1860s; their languages, dialects, and accents varied over time and place, changing as they interacted with other black people as well as with whites and Native Americans. Five of the first eleven African men who arrived in Dutch New Amsterdam in 1626—Paul d'Angola, Simon Congo, Anthony Portuguese, John Francisco, and Gracia Angola—had spent enough time among the Portuguese on the Angolan coast or on ships to have acquired Christian first names and Portuguese last names. Some of the enslaved people whose labor created the Carolina gold rice came from Barbados and carried with them the accents and words of that Caribbean island. And Sojourner Truth, who became an abolitionist and preacher, was born in a Dutch settlement in upstate New York in the 1790s and spoke only Dutch until she was sold, at age nine, to an English-speaking owner. Her inability to understand the English commands of her new mistress brought whippings for the child, so she would have quickly learned the new language.

Eighteenth-century newspaper advertisements, which sought the capture and return of runaway slaves, often commented on the language spoken by the errant slave. Some ads said the runaway spoke "good English." Some noted that he or she spoke little or no English, and some identified the other language the person spoke.

An ad in the *New York Gazette* in 1748, for example, searched for a "Spanish Negro Man, named Domingo" whom the owners said "speaks bad English." In other New York ads, an owner claimed that Clause, who ran away at age twenty-seven, played the fiddle and spoke English and Dutch; Lucretia's owner said that she had not been in the country for long but spoke broken English and Dutch. In 1764, an owner in Albany reported that his runaway slave, Jacob, "speaks good English, some French and a little Spanish, but little or no Dutch." In 1780, Lucas Von Beverholdt of New Jersey searched for "a negro man named Jack" who spoke "broken English and some Negro Dutch," this latter was presumably a Dutch dialect that Africans in America had created. And in 1796, an owner in North Carolina advertised for the capture and return of two men, both of whom spoke English and French. Why these men spoke French in a colony that had always been English is not clear. Their owner suspected that they would attempt to get onto a ship headed to the West Indies so perhaps they had come to America during the Haitian Revolution.

Being multilingual was, of course, more prevalent in the early colonial period when the Dutch, Spanish, French, and Portuguese had more of a presence and influence in America, and while people were being brought into the country as slaves directly from Africa or from the Caribbean. However, variations in dialect, accent, and language remained a reality throughout the entire period of slavery as people moved about through the domestic slave trade. For example, during the antebellum period when English became the dominant language, a young person sold from the Upper South states of Virginia or Maryland to New Orleans or Charleston in the Lower South would have spoken differently over time, incorporating regional dialects and intonations as she adjusted to new surroundings with different cultural and linguistic influences.

Captives refashioned their African languages with European languages to create new tongues. In Haiti, they created a creole;

in Jamaica, or creole; and in Georgia and South Carolina, they created the creole language of Gullah. Linguists and historians have recently concluded that the Gullah language spoken by people in South Carolina and Georgia bears a strong resemblance to the Fula dialect from Sierra Leone, a country on the grain coast of West Africa from which captives were taken. Because Africans and their descendants on the Sea Islands of South Carolina and Georgia tended to live on large plantations where they were relatively isolated from white owners, Gullah language and culture was able to develop and survive for centuries. Indeed, Gullah is still spoken today by many of the descendants of those original slaves.

Most enslaved people did not live on islands or peninsulas far removed from large populations of whites, but nonetheless they tended to live in communities with other black people, thus enabling them to create, sustain, and pass on African American dialects and other cultural practices. It is true that enslaved people in northern colonies in the early decades of slavery often lived with and worked alongside their owners. And in the South, in both the colonial and antebellum periods, some enslaved people lived on small farms or in urban settings where they interacted with whites and did not live among large communities of black people. In the antebellum South, though, the majority of enslaved people lived on plantations with more than twenty slaves. Although most whites in the antebellum South either owned no slaves or fewer than five, large planters owned the vast majority of enslaved people. In the antebellum South, then, the majority of slaves lived in communities of other slaves and in close proximity to free black people.

On large plantations, the degree of interaction with white owners varied, depending on the role of the enslaved person. People who worked in the owners' home as cooks, launderers, or butlers may have lived inside the home or in a nearby space. Sometimes the cook lived above the kitchen, which was usually in a separate building yet very close to the owner's house. Sometimes, as at Boone Hall Plantation, owners constructed a row of cabins for enslaved artisans near the owner's home. In this way, visitors could view the cabins as they drove in their carriages down the long oak-canopied pathway leading to the house. Such close proximity subjected them to close scrutiny from the white family, and some were on call to meet the owner's needs at any time of the day and night. Still, although they lived away from the larger population of slaves in slave quarters near the fields, these enslaved people likely interacted with the field hands and participated in the activities of the larger slave community at Boone Hall. Within such communities enslaved people formed bonds with one another; they created practices, beliefs, and rituals, all of which provided them respite and enjoyment, and helped them to survive their captivity.

To be sure, slave communities were no more idyllic than any others. Close contact in small cabins and in crowded slave quarters could generate conflicts among enslaved people. They, like anyone else, experienced jealousy, betrayal, dislike, and conflicting or competing beliefs. A fellow slave might provide information to owners about where a runaway had gone, or might betray a plot to rebel. Women and men, both those who were forced into relationships by owners and those who had entered into consensual relationships, could reach the point where they wanted to be apart.

Within slave communities the cabin was the center of family life; groups of cabins formed the larger slave quarters. Archaeological excavations provide information about the size of long-decayed cabins, the placement of fireplaces and chimneys, and the proximity of cabins to each other and to the owner's house. The size and type of cabin varied over time and location, but two types predominated in the antebellum period: a single family structure measuring sixteen by twenty feet, and a two-family double cabin that measured twenty by forty feet with a common wall that

8. Original wooden slave cabins at McLeod Plantation, on James Island, South Carolina. Cabins served as the center of family life for most enslaved people.

separated one family's space from the other. Cabins were constructed from various types of material including wood; tabby, a sort of cement made by crushing oyster shells into lime and mixing it with sand and water; and finally, brick. Enslaved workers usually made the bricks for the cabins right there on the plantation, as they did at the Stagville and Boone Hall plantations.

Cabins generally had a wooden window without glass, and a fireplace that residents used for heating as well as for cooking. The cabins were hot in the summer, cold in the winter, and dark even in the daytime. People sometimes built a bed by covering a board with straw, but most often they slept on pallets or on the floor. A family's space consisted of one room in which as many as eight or nine people lived. In addition to family members, an owner might assign an unrelated child or adult to live in a cabin, perhaps someone who had been recently purchased. In some cabins, there were no families at all, but instead numerous single people who shared the same small space.

Excavations have also yielded objects that both offer suggestions and raise questions about how people lived. For example, archaeologists have found a few cowrie shells that were used for trade in parts of West Africa, prompting questions about how the shells got there and what significance they held for the people who owned them. Shards of European ceramics raise questions about how enslaved people in a particular cabin got hold of a ceramic cup or plate that one might expect to find in a wealthy person's home. Digs have found clay pipes used for smoking tobacco and have identified colonoware pottery, hand-made, unglazed earthenware once thought to have been made only by Native Americans, which suggests that African Americans also crafted pottery from mud and clay.

Archaeology also provides insight into which foods people ate and how they prepared these. Enslaved people used the parts of animals that whites did not want, such as skulls, feet, and ribs, but there was some differentiation among slaves even on the same plantation and people considered more skilled or valuable may have received meat that was more similar to what the owners ate. Remains of bones found under owners' homes and slave cabins, and the knife markings on them demonstrate that plantation owners ate larger cuts of roasted meat, while enslaved people tended to have small cuts, which they cooked in stews. Bones also suggest that enslaved people provided a substantial amount of their own food, such as animals and seafood that they caught in order to supplement their diets. Domestic animals such as pigs, cows, sheep, and goats supplied most of the protein in slaves' diets. Other unearthed remains include crabs, clams, oysters, turtles, fish, opossum, raccoon, and rabbit that had been trapped in the woods or caught with nets in the ocean, or in rivers and creeks. Slaves rarely ate chicken; remains of deer, other wild animals, and birds or ducks have rarely been found, likely because slaves had limited or no access to firearms due to legislation inspired by fear of insurrection.

The people who lived in the cabins formed families despite the absence of any legal recognition of marriage among them. Henry Bibb, who escaped slavery and made his way to Canada, wrote in the narrative of his life, "There is no legal marriage among the slaves of the South. I never saw nor heard of such a thing in my life, and I have been through seven of the slave states. A slave marrying according to law, is a thing unknown in the history of American Slavery." Bibb was correct. The law did not recognize legal marriage among slaves because enslaved people were considered property; as such they had no ability to enter into legal contracts. Still, enslaved men and women formed relationships that they considered marriage. Many people chose partners whom they cared about; others had no choice and were assigned partners whom the owner selected for them. Owners considered it to their benefit to have enslaved people living in marriage-like relationships for at least two reasons. First, they would be more likely to produce children who would belong to the mother's owner. Second, owners thought that people who were part of a family were much less likely to attempt to escape, leaving their loved ones behind. Marriage then, even in this limited form, lent a kind of stability to slavery in the owners' eyes though they always reserved the right to break up marriages and families by selling or giving away the people they owned.

Many people engaged in what they and owners termed "abroad marriages," in which the woman and man belonged to different owners. Enslaved people insisted on these arrangements in part because they wanted to be careful not to marry their cousins. But many owners considered abroad marriage a threat to their control over the people they owned. Usually the husband traveled from his plantation to the cabin of his wife and children. Owners generally permitted this movement once or twice per week, but sometimes the man wanted to visit more frequently. Owners of the men complained that they risked losing work time from these men. On the women's plantations, owners complained that husbands strolled onto their property in the middle of the day while the slaves on the plantation were supposed to be at work. Such men, they argued, set a bad example and threatened to disrupt the flow of work on the wife's plantation. Abroad marriages constituted a continuing source of tension between owners and slaves, even though a few owners were known to have purchased a mate for a slave so that he could have control over both of them or to promote peace on the plantation.

In addition to nuclear families with both parents living together or the father or mother living on a neighboring plantation, other family constellations existed. For example, as a young boy Frederick Douglass lived with his grandparents on a plantation in Maryland, which was owned by a white man rumored to be Douglass's father but with whom he had no relationship. Douglass's mother was hired out about twelve miles from the plantation and surreptitiously visited her son. "She made her journeys to see me in the night, travelling the whole distance on foot, after the performance of her day's work," Douglass wrote. "She was a field hand, and a whipping is the penalty of not being in the field at sunrise, unless a slave has special permission from his or her master to the contrary—a permission which they seldom get. . . . I do not recollect of ever seeing my mother by the light of day. She was with me in the night. She would lie down with me, and get me to sleep, but long before I waked she was gone. Very little communication ever took place between us." Douglass and his mother were separated when he was an infant; she died when he was about seven years old. He never lived with her and saw her only late at night on a few occasions. Douglass spent his formative years among an extended family that included his grandparents, his aunt, and several young cousins. According to Douglass, his Grandmother Betsey took care of the children as their mothers were hired out far away. His grandmother's "kindness and love," he said, stood in place of his mother's.

Marriage, and more broadly, family, did in fact help to make life more bearable for the enslaved people. As owners suspected, being married made it less likely that an enslaved person would run away. Indeed, the majority of people who escaped were young single men, who while they may have left parents, siblings, and extended family behind, did not have wives or children of their own. Caring about family members helped to give meaning to life and created significant emotional connections that could distract from and ameliorate the pain of the labor and the violence of slavery. In the small cabins where families spent time together, parents told their children stories about their African ancestry, or about family members from whom they had been separated, or about their memories of growing up. They taught them how to work, and how to interact with owners and with other enslaved people.

Having a family could add meaning to life, but it could also bring about grief. Families and communities were frequently disrupted through sale, movement of owners, or the indebtedness of owners who held absolute power to dispose of slaves as they pleased. Families experienced separation because owners relocated, taking some slaves with them, leaving some behind. Sometimes an enslaved person was given as a wedding gift and taken far away. And the death of an owner frequently brought about the separation of enslaved families and communities as heirs arrived to claim the people an owner had bequeathed to them. Most often, though, enslaved people experienced the loss of family through sale as part of the domestic slave trade.

In the cabins and the quarters, people found the emotional space to express their fears, their resentment, and their hopes among other slaves who shared the same anxieties. When people got news of an owner's impending death, or learned of his serious debt, they whispered in the quarters about what would become of them. They turned to one another as they wondered if family members would be sold separately, if people who had worked closely on a gang would be divided, and if anything would remain of their community. Not every enslaved person experienced sale and separation personally, but many adults lived with the knowledge of their vulnerability and threat of separation.

Life within the small cabins spilled out easily into the common areas of the slave quarters. People worked closely together, particularly on plantations that employed the gang system. They knew each other well through their labor; they also spent a good deal of time together in the social life of the slave quarters. Some built cooking fires outside of the cabins and ate communal meals with other enslaved people. Groups of people, particularly men and boys, went off to fish or crab or to catch oysters. Women washed clothes in the yards of the quarters, and inside the cabins they gathered to help each other to sew scraps of cloth into the quilts that kept their families warm.

At night and on Sundays they attended religious services or entertained themselves. People danced to the music of banjos (mbanza), which Africans had introduced to colonial America, based on their memories of similar instruments in West and Central Africa. Some played bones and drums, also derived from African instruments. And others played the fiddles they adopted from Europeans. Folk tales, like that of Anansi, the trickster spider who always prevailed over others much more powerful than he, spread throughout the enslaved populations on plantations. Anansi, like the banjo, had accompanied African captives to the Americas, and they shaped the stories to fit the circumstances in which they found themselves in places like Jamaica, Suriname, and the American South. People told jokes that sometimes aimed at their subjection. One, for example, revealed a belief that slave owners would be punished for enslaving African Americans: An owner told his slave that he would reward him by having him buried in the vault with the owner. The enslaved man replied, "On the one hand I'm happy about having a good coffin, on the other hand, I'm afraid that when the devil comes to get you, he may take me by mistake." Although said in humor, this story reflected a belief among many enslaved people, that there would have to be divine justice in the end, which meant there would be no room in heaven for whites who had benefitted from enslaving blacks. In this belief, they echoed David Walker's question, "Is God not a God of Justice?"

Christianity was supposed to encourage docility, but for some people it justified equality. Many rejected the interpretations of Christianity that owners sought to force on them and held on to the promises they extrapolated from the Bible, believing that they would be delivered from slavery; that there was a better place beyond the world in which they worked against their will, lost their families, and suffered from violence at the hands of owners, overseers, and drivers. These people found comfort in the words of the Bible, and they created a music that expressed their theology. These spiritual songs or spirituals applied biblical stories of liberation and consolation to the conditions under which enslaved, and some free black people lived.

> Didn't my Lord deliver Daniel
> Deliver Daniel, deliver Daniel
> Didn't my Lord deliver Daniel
> An' why not-a every man.
> He delivered Daniel from the lion's den
> Jonah from the belly of the whale
> An' the Hebrew chillun from the fiery furnace
> An' why not every man.

God had worked miracles in the past, why wouldn't he work them now for his children held in captivity in America?

For those in physical or psychic pain, there was the assurance of a balm in Gilead.

> Sometimes I feel discouraged, and think my work's in vain,
> But then the Holy Spirit revives my soul again.

There is a balm in Gilead to make the wounded whole,
There is a balm in Gilead to heal the sin-sick soul.

If you cannot preach like Peter, if you cannot pray like Paul,
You can tell the love of Jesus and say, "He died for all."
There is a balm in Gilead to make the wounded whole,
There is a balm in Gilead to heal the sin-sick soul.

Enslaved people also drew upon hymns that white Americans and Europeans composed, so that when Bethany Veney stood on an auction block in a Richmond, Virginia, slave market, she hung on to the promises of love and support provided in a hymn she had learned at the Methodist meetings she attended with her owner's relatives.

When through the deep waters I call thee to go,
The rivers of woe shall not thee overflow;
For I will be with thee, and cause thee to stand,
Upheld by my righteous, omnipotent hand.

And when slave traders led people away, other enslaved people left the fields and sang hymns in which pain and hope merged.

When we all meet in heaven
There is no parting there;
When we all meet in heaven
There is parting no more.

People incorporated their hopes and beliefs into the songs that they sang or hummed not only in church but also in the cabins, around the quarters, in their places of work, in the fields, and at points of sale and separation. This was one of the ways in which they drew upon religion to help them to survive slavery. Frederick Douglass, when he wrote of the songs that he had heard other enslaved people sing, spoke of the sorrow and the hope embedded within them. "They told a tale of woe," he wrote, "which was then altogether beyond my feeble comprehension; they were tones loud, long, and deep; they breathed the prayer and complaint of souls boiling over with the bitterest anguish. Every tone was a testimony against slavery, and a prayer to God for deliverance from chains." These tones, these testimonies, created in communities of slaves, helped to sustain some through the centuries of captivity.

Chapter 6
Taking slavery apart

Slavery existed in America for nearly two hundred and fifty years until it was finally abolished with the ratification of the Thirteenth Amendment in December 1865. It took all those years and a civil war to end slavery, but many enslaved people had made attempts all along to destroy it. Whether they did so in an effort to gain individual freedom by escaping, or by negotiating ways to ameliorate their enslavement, or by participating in violent uprisings, some African Americans always challenged the system that named them as property and denied them the rights of other human beings. But challenging slavery, even while it was being put into place, was a difficult feat, and as the institution matured and proved more and more lucrative, it became even more impervious to resistance. The first eleven slaves in New Amsterdam had negotiated a degree of freedom for themselves and their wives, but they were unable to extend those privileges to their children. The participants in the Stono Rebellion set out to attain promised freedom in Florida, but their efforts were quickly thwarted. Nat Turner and his conspirators made a strike for freedom, but their rebellion was suppressed and despite debates in the Virginia legislature about ending slavery, lawmakers preserved the institution and imposed even more severe restrictions on enslaved people. Beginning in the early 1700s, some whites, primarily Quakers, also spoke against and took action to end slavery. Abolition finally came in the nineteenth century after both African Americans and groups of whites forcefully challenged the system of slavery on moral grounds and threatened the political power of white southerners who fought back to protect the wealth they held in human beings.

Prior to the Civil War, the most sustained and successful effort to take slavery apart occurred during the American Revolution. The Revolutionary War, in which some white Americans in the thirteen colonies made a claim for political liberty against England, ended up leading to freedom for thousands of Africans and African Americans as they escaped from slavery, and northern colonies moved to abolish the institution within their borders. As American whites articulated a language of freedom and liberty with regard to England, some enslaved people adopted that language to argue for their own freedom from whites. The Revolutionary War brought about freedom for some African Americans, but the Constitution locked slavery into place in the South, where the institution continued to expand, justified on political, social, and religious grounds. The Revolutionary era pushed American colonial society in conflicting directions and made plain some of the contradictions contained in ideologies of liberty in a place where slavery thrived.

Perhaps as a portent that the Revolution would have implications for African Americans, the first man to die in that war was Crispus Attucks, a runaway slave from Boston. After the English Parliament passed legislation in the 1760s that taxed Americans to help defray the costs of the Seven Years War, tensions were high in the American colonies, particularly in Massachusetts, where armed English soldiers still stood guard. On a Monday night in March 1770, a group of men surrounded a British soldier, taunting him. Other soldiers came to his aid. The colonists pelted the soldiers with snowballs and pieces of ice, accusing the first soldier of having used the butt of his musket on a boy who had insulted him. Things escalated and the soldiers fired into the crowd. Five men fell dead in what is known as the Boston Massacre.

Among the dead was Crispus Attucks, the first man killed in the American Revolution. According to the testimony of an enslaved man who was an eyewitness, Attucks had struck at the soldiers with a club.

In 1750 Attucks had been the subject of a runaway slave ad. William Brown advertised for the capture of an escaped slave, "a mulatto fellow, about 27 years of age, named Crispus, 6 feet 2 inches high, short, curled hair, his knees nearer together than common." Attucks, who was descended from Africans and Wampanoag Indians, had since worked on ships in the Boston Harbor. Some reports say that he ate in a tavern that night and led the crowd of colonists to the soldier. He was not the only black man in the crowd; one pro-British witness described the mob as "saucy boys, Negroes and mulattoes, Irish Teagues and outlandish Jack Tars [sailors]." It is not clear what motivated Attucks to taunt the English soldiers, but the fact that this first man to die was black and legally a slave, physically connected the colonial struggle against England for independence with blacks' struggle to be free. Attucks became a martyr of the Revolution. Despite being black, he was buried, along with some of the other men who died that night, in a cemetery reserved for honored dead.

Other black people were determined to insert themselves and their status as slaves into this Revolutionary-era conversation about liberty. Slavery had hardened as an institution over the course of the eighteenth century, but now black people perceived talk of revolution as a way of gaining freedom. As white American men rhetorically posited themselves as slaves who were claiming their freedom from England, African Americans became increasingly forthright in applying the language of liberty and natural rights to their situation. A decided tension developed between the notion of property in people and notions of liberty, and African-descended people began to identify their own liberty with the claims of liberty that white men asserted in their challenge to England.

In April 1773, four slaves in Boston sent a petition to the legislature urging that they be set free so that they could return to Africa. They referred to the conflict between Britain and the colonies as supporting their request. "We expect great things from men who have made such a noble stand against the designs of their *fellow-men* to enslave them," the petition read. The enslaved men asked the legislators to keep in mind white Americans' own struggle for liberty when they considered the appeal.

At the May 1774 session of the Massachusetts legislature, several enslaved men again petitioned for their freedom. They described themselves as a "Grate number of blacks of this Province who are held in a State of Slavery within the bowels of a free and Christian country.... Your petitioners," they continued, "apprehend we have in common with all other men a natural right to our freedom without being deprived of them by our fellow men as we are a freeborn people and have never forfeited this Blessing by any compact or agreement whatever." They pleaded for gradual emancipation that would bring about freedom for all then in bondage when they reached the age of twenty-one. Six weeks later they followed up the appeal with a request for "some part of the unimproved land, belonging to the province, for a settlement, that each of us may there sit down quietly under his own fig tree." None of the petitions was granted.

African Americans attempted to connect their status as slaves to the war both rhetorically and tactically, but in July 1775, when George Washington organized the Continental Army, he forbade the enlistment of black men, whether free or slave, and the reenlistment of the black men who had served at Lexington, Concord, Bunker Hill, and in other battles. All thirteen colonies followed Washington's example; patriot leaders feared that allowing African American men to enlist would encourage them to leave their owners.

In November 1775, Virginia's royal governor, Lord Dunmore, opted to use the resources that George Washington rejected. Dunmore understood that some enslaved African Americans would be willing to fight for the English if doing so would guarantee their freedom. Indeed, earlier that year, three enslaved men had presented themselves to Dunmore with just such an offer. He rejected them at that time but later realized how disruptive it would be to Virginia planters (who depended on slave labor to produce their wealth) to have their slaves armed against them.

The proclamation promised freedom to slaves whose owners favored separating from England; Dunmore intended to use these slaves to subdue their owners. The Virginia Assembly responded with its own declaration that threatened to put to death any black person, free or slave, who joined with the English. "We think it proper to declare, that all slaves who have been, or shall be seduced, by his lordship's proclamation, or other arts, to desert their masters' service, and take up arms against the inhabitants of this colony, shall be liable to such punishment," the Virginia proclamation stated. The assembly promised to pardon any slaves who put down their arms and returned to owners. Still, thousands of enslaved men, women, and children risked their lives in efforts to get to the British lines; the men who made it through were inducted into Lord Dunmore's Ethiopian Regiment and wore uniforms that bore the motto "Liberty to Slaves."

Fearful of the consequences if enslaved people fought against their owners, George Washington now shifted his position and sought to minimize the impact of black men fighting for the British. On December 26, 1775, he wrote about Dunmore, "If that man is not crushed before the Spring he will become the most dangerous man in America. His strength will increase like a snowball running down hill. Success will depend on which side can arm the Negro faster." Washington then allowed African American men to enlist in the Continental Army. The Continental Congress initially resisted this move for fear of alienating slaveholders, but by the end of 1776 troop shortages led them and colonial governments to recruit black men.

Northern colonies implemented this new policy first. New York, New Jersey, and Connecticut enabled owners to free their slaves to serve as substitutes for them and their sons. All the other northern colonies and the middle colonies followed. South Carolina, on the other hand, never allowed black men to enlist although this did not stop them from leaving Carolina and enlisting in other colonies or with the British. In the end, of course, the British lost. In 1783 nearly four thousand black people sailed from New York under the protection of the British Navy. About fourteen thousand black people in all left with the British. Most had not served directly but had sought refuge. Some ended up in England, Nova Scotia, Canada, Sierra Leone, or West Africa. One small group went to Trinidad, where they were allowed to form a free community even though slavery existed there. Most of the more than five thousand black men who fought on the side of the Americans also received their freedom, vastly increasing the number of free black people in the new states.

The language of liberty and freedom struck not only African Americans as contradictory and discordant with the existence of slavery in America. In this era of revolution, some whites also began to think that the actual physical enslavement of people could not be reconciled with values of liberty and independence. Two examples depict the concern.

September 1774: Abigail Adams wrote to her husband, John Adams, and told him about the discovery of a widespread plot of rebellion among slaves in Boston: "I wish most sincerely that there was not a slave in the province.... It always appeared a most iniquitous scheme to me to fight ourselves for what we are daily robbing and plundering from those who have as good a right to freedom as we have."

1754–1776: Quakers, a few of whom had since the founding of the religion in the late 1600s, condemned the violence and immorality of slavery, officially turned their backs on the institution during

the Revolutionary era. The Philadelphia Yearly Meeting of
Friends that presided over Quakers in Pennsylvania, New Jersey,
Delaware, and Maryland, with the urging of a minister John
Woolman and a teacher Anthony Benezet, had renounced
slavery in 1754. Subsequently, some Quakers freed their slaves, but
most did not. In 1776, the year of America's Declaration of
Independence, the Yearly Meeting decided to prohibit slave
ownership among its members.

In 1780: Massachusetts adopted its own constitution with
significant ramifications for enslaved people. Its declaration of
rights read: "All men are born free and equal, and have certain
natural, essential, and unalienable rights; among which may be
reckoned the right of enjoying and defending their lives and
liberties; that of acquiring, possessing, and protecting property; in
fine, that of seeking and obtaining their safety and happiness."
African Americans in Massachusetts quickly moved to apply these
rights to their condition. Slave owners used slavery as a metaphor
for their relationship to England, but these African Americans
pointed to the reality of their own enslavement and reasoned that
they had as much right as whites to be free.

May 1781: In Berkshire County, Massachusetts, an enslaved
woman named Bett, also called Mum Bett, and an enslaved man
named Brom sued for their freedom from John Ashley, a judge in
the county, alleging that they were free because the new state
constitution outlawed slavery. The jury held that the two were not
Ashley's property, and the court awarded them damages. Ashley
filed an appeal of the decision but did not pursue it, possibly
because another court in Massachusetts had also handed down a
ruling of freedom in the case of Quock Walker. Walker sued his
owner not only on grounds of criminal assault and battery but also
on the claim that his former owner had promised to free him
when he reached the age of twenty-five. While appeals in those
civil cases were pending, the attorney general prosecuted Walker's
owner on the assault and battery charges. In his jury instructions,

the judge invoked the new state constitution that declared all men are born free and equal and entitled to liberty. "Slavery," he said, "is in my judgment as effectively abolished as it can be by the granting of rights and privileges wholly incompatible and repugnant to its existence. The courts are therefore fully of the opinion that perpetual servitude can no longer be tolerated in our government and that liberty can only be forfeited by some criminal conduct or relinquished by personal consent or contract." As the plaintiffs' attorneys had urged, this judge declared that slavery could not exist alongside the new constitution's broad claims of equality and freedom.

A judge's charge to a jury does not typically create state law, but it was becoming clear to both slaves and slave owners in Massachusetts that slavery would not stand up to legal challenge within the state. The courts' rulings created an atmosphere that discouraged slavery, and by the time of the 1790 census, there were no slaves living in Massachusetts. Mum Bett spent the rest of her life working as a free woman in her attorney's household. In her last will and testament she listed her name as Elizabeth Freeman.

Unlike Massachusetts, where emancipation took place fairly quickly, other states undertook a process of gradual emancipation. With pressure from Quakers, Pennsylvania passed a law in 1780 that freed all black people born after passage of the law but not until they reached the age of twenty-eight. According to the law they would gain freedom in 1808. Connecticut passed a law in 1784 that manumitted slaves born that year but required that they serve as indentured servants until the age of twenty-five. This meant that they would not be fully free until 1809. Rhode Island made the same provision in 1784. In New York and New Jersey, where the economy depended more on slave labor, freedom came even more slowly. After heated debates among abolitionists and proslavery advocates, New York's gradual emancipation plan began in 1799, and the last slaves gained their freedom in 1827. New Jersey adopted its plan in 1804, but its law provided for long-lasting "apprenticeships" that were possibly more like slavery than freedom.

As some northern states began the process of emancipating slaves, representatives on the federal level met and formulated the Constitution that would govern the United States of America. Again, the potential existed to eliminate slavery all together, and delegates to the Constitutional Convention debated the possibility. In spring 1787, fifty-five men met in Philadelphia to consider the shortcomings of the Articles of Confederation. These were men of high social status, with no artisans, laborers or even middling farmers among them. Two-thirds of the delegates were lawyers, seven had been governors and twenty-five were slave owners. Among the delegates were James Madison, Alexander Hamilton, Benjamin Franklin, and George Washington who was elected to preside over the meeting. The Convention was charged with revising the Articles of Confederation that had been put into place during the Revolution as the separate colonies bound themselves together to fight against England. However, the delegates eventually created a new constitution that laid out the rights and obligations of citizens and kept slavery alive in the new country. Without ever using the words slave or slavery, the document addressed enslaved people and the institution of slavery in three ways: through the "three-fifths clause" regarding Congressional representation; by setting a date after which Congress could outlaw the Atlantic slave trade; and by providing for the return of fugitive slaves to their owners.

Delegates debated the issue of whether slaves should be counted toward a state's population in order to determine the number of representatives in Congress. Southern states argued that slaves should count; northern states that were freeing slaves disagreed because this would result in a distortion of power based on people who were not citizens but property. There was a great deal at stake. Enumerating slaves in the population would determine not only the number of representatives but also electoral votes in selecting the President. The Convention reached a compromise, and using euphemistic language, in article 1, section 2, agreed that all free persons, plus "three fifths of all other Persons" would constitute the numerical base for the apportionment of representatives. The term "all other persons" referred to enslaved African Americans. Perceiving a threat from northern states to the continued existence of slavery, southern delegates wanted to dominate in Congress and in the Electoral College in order to keep slavery intact. Counting slaves to determine representation helped them to do that. Indeed, from 1801 until 1861, only one president, John Quincy Adams, opposed slavery. All the others were either slave owners themselves, or supporters of slavery.

The convention next addressed whether to abolish America's participation in the Atlantic slave trade. By 1787, when the Constitution was being drafted, ten states had already outlawed the importation of slaves. Georgia, South Carolina, and North Carolina had not done so, and their delegates threatened to leave the Convention if the trade were banned. If slavery was threatened, they said, there would be no Union. Charles Pinckney, a delegate from South Carolina, argued, "South Carolina and Georgia cannot do without slaves." Further, he presciently predicted that if slaves could no longer be brought into the country, planters in Upper South states such as Virginia and Maryland would gain by trading their surplus slaves to the Deep South. He further contended that continuation of the Atlantic slave trade would benefit the entire country economically as ships from the North participated in the trade, and the federal government would gain more revenue for the treasury through taxation of the goods slaves produced. Delegates once again compromised. In article 1, section 9, the Constitution provided that Congress would have the power to ban the international slave trade but not until 1808—twenty years later. Southern states took full advantage of this grace period by bringing in large numbers of captives. South Carolina alone imported more than forty thousand slaves over the next twenty years. As one North Carolina delegate to the Constitutional Convention stated, Georgia and South Carolina had lost a great many slaves during the Revolutionary War, but over the course of the next twenty years they would be fully supplied with enslaved persons.

Finally, the delegates considered an issue that was becoming more and more relevant as northern states abolished slavery: that of the rights of owners with regard to slaves who escaped. Delegates could see that such states as Pennsylvania, New York, and Massachusetts would become havens for those who wanted to escape slavery in the South, so they put in place a fugitive slave clause. Article 4, section 2 provided: "No person held to service or labor in one State, under the laws thereof, escaping into another, shall, in consequence of any law or regulation therein, be discharged from such service or labor, but shall be delivered up on claim of the party to whom such service or labor may be due." Slaves who escaped and reached a free state would not be legally free and could be returned to their owners.

With these three provisions, the U.S. Constitution accepted slavery as a valid institution in the new nation, thereby inserting the federal government into the role of regulating slavery. But the Revolution had made a great difference, and, going forward, most of those who opposed slavery drew upon the Constitution's language of justice and liberty to advocate for the abolition of slavery in America. The values expressed in such rhetoric amounted to a vivid contradiction to slavery; throughout the nineteenth century black and white abolitionists demanded the fulfillment of the promises of the founding documents.

In the years following the Revolution and ratification of the Constitution, slavery diminished and eventually disappeared in the northern states of New Hampshire, Massachusetts, Rhode Island, Connecticut, New York, New Jersey, and Pennsylvania. Some owners in the Upper South also freed their slaves. Simultaneously, slavery grew in the Lower South. Between 1800 and 1810 the number of enslaved people expanded by 33 percent, due in part to importation of slaves from Africa and the Caribbean, and in part to reproduction. In 1808 Congress took the opportunity provided in the Constitution to abolish the Atlantic slave trade. England, prodded by the insistence of abolitionists, had outlawed its participation in the trade the year before.

Once free, African Americans in northern states faced prejudice and discrimination from whites. Many black former slaves worked at low-paying jobs, lived in squalid conditions, and had little or no access to education for themselves or their children. When David Walker challenged free blacks to look at the quality of their freedom, *this* is what he meant. He wanted them to realize that they were only slightly removed from the condition of enslavement and therefore had a vested interest in helping to bring about freedom for slaves as well as equal treatment for all people of color. Beginning in the late 1700s, African Americans in the North organized to obtain political and civil rights. In Philadelphia, New York, and Boston they established schools and other self-help organizations. In 1794, Richard Allen and other black men formed the African Methodist Episcopal Church out of anger and frustration with their treatment as inferior beings by white Methodist Church members.

In the South too, there were always free black people who had purchased their freedom or had been manumitted by owners, often in their wills. Most lived under severe restrictions. Conditions for them varied according to where they lived, so that life in a city such as Charleston provided more opportunities than living in a small town or rural area. Other cities, such as Savannah, required that a free person of color have a white guardian who would vouch for him or her. Often, legislation that regulated black behavior included both enslaved and free black people. Free and enslaved blacks interacted often, since some were related through birth or marriage; to many whites, these close interactions posed a threat to the stability of slavery.

In 1816 a group of prominent white statesmen devised a controversial response to having enslaved and free blacks in America. The group launched the American Colonization Society to encourage manumission of slaves and emigration of free black people to what became Liberia, a territory on the west coast of Africa. The group included Francis Scott Key, Andrew Jackson, Daniel Webster, and Henry Clay, the congressman from Kentucky and Speaker of the House of Representatives. Among the members were antislavery men who wanted to see an end to slavery, as well as slave owners who wanted to rid America of free black people.

But by the 1820s most black people had been born in America; many came from families that had been in the country for generations. Still, some black abolitionists including James Grimké of Philadelphia, who had become wealthy through his invention of a type of sail, at first supported the idea of emigration. He viewed it not just as a way to encourage manumission of slaves but also believed that African Americans would never be able to progress while living among whites in America. Both black leaders and white abolitionists soon rejected the scheme, however, and came to believe that the main intention was simply to rid the country of free black people. Fewer than ten thousand emigrated to Liberia between 1820 and 1856.

Instead of focusing on removing free people from this country, in the 1820s abolitionists intensified their call for immediate rather than gradual abolition in the United States. The call first went out from abolitionists in England who fought for an end to slavery in the Caribbean colonies. In 1824, the English Quaker Elizabeth Heyrick published a pamphlet *Immediate Not Gradual Abolition: Or, An Inquiry Into the Shortest, Safest, and Most Effectual Means of Getting Rid of West Indian Slavery.* In the pamphlet she argued that although seventeen years had passed since the abolition of the Atlantic slave trade, slavery still flourished in the English

colonies. Each individual had to take responsibility for the sin
and shame of slavery. "The West Indian planter and the people
of this country, stand in the same moral relation to each other as
the thief and the receiver of stolen goods," she argued, and she
called for a boycott of sugar and other commodities that slaves
produced in the West Indies. Some American abolitionists later
adopted this strategy of boycotting goods produced by enslaved
people.

In America, five years after Heyrick's pamphlet, David Walker
published his *Appeal* in which he decried colonization efforts as "a
plan got up by a gang of slave-holders to select the free people of
colour from among the slaves, that our more miserable brethren
may be the better secured in ignorance and wretchedness, to work
their farms and dig their mines, and thus go on enriching the
Christians with their blood and groans."

Walker rejected the argument that colonization would clear
America of some of its moral debt by asking the question: "[Are]
Americans innocent of the blood and groans of our fathers and us,
their children? Every individual may plead innocence, if he
pleases, but God will, before long, separate the innocent from the
guilty, unless something is speedily done—which I suppose will
hardly be, so that their destruction may be sure."

It was exactly this fear of divine damnation and destruction as
punishment for individual and national sin that inspired some
white evangelical Christians to take up the cause of abolition. At
revivals during the Second Great Awakening from the turn of the
nineteenth century to the late 1830s, ministers preached messages
of immediate repentance and conversion, and called for Christians
to put their beliefs into action by performing good works. Out of
this evangelical movement emerged white Christians who
supported several reform movements including abolition and
temperance. These abolitionists believed that just as individuals
could repent of sin, so too could America repent of the sin of

slavery; just as individuals could work out their own salvation, so too could they take the steps to eradicate the sin of slavery. In the 1830s, several groups of people including ardent white believers, black abolitionists, some of whom had escaped from slavery, and enslaved people who violently rebelled against slavery, pushed the abolition movement to more broadly embrace the call for immediate emancipation.

Three major events occurred in 1831 that had immense impact on the movement to end slavery. On January 1, William Lloyd Garrison, a white man who had grown up in poverty in Massachusetts, published the first issue of his abolitionist newspaper, the *Liberator*, and launched his obstinate call for immediate, rather than gradual abolition. Garrison had been influenced to embrace abolition when he worked with a white Quaker and boarded with a free black family in Baltimore, Maryland, where he also saw slavery firsthand. He at first supported colonization, but by 1831 rejected it as inadequate and injurious to the cause of freedom.

In August, Nat Turner led the bloody slave rebellion in Southampton County, Virginia. And then, in December, enslaved people rose up in a mass rebellion in Jamaica, the English colony in the West Indies. Again, this revolt struck fear in the hearts of people who owned or lived among slaves in Jamaica, America, and elsewhere in the Atlantic world. By 1833 England had abolished slavery in its West Indian colonies. Each of these events of 1831 intensified the arguments for and against slavery, spurring both abolitionists and supporters of slavery to expand the realm of their influence.

By establishing antislavery societies, publishing newspapers, books, and pamphlets, giving speeches in America and in England, devising strategies, and filing petitions in Congress, black and white abolitionists worked to destroy slavery. Former slaves dictated or wrote narratives of their experiences, highlighting the violence and moral decay of owners and traders, and these narratives inspired northerners to challenge the institution itself. Frederick Douglass, Lydia Maria Child, Rev. J. W. Pennington, Sarah and Angelina Grimké, James Forten, Theodore Weld, and numerous other black and white men and women challenged the powerful institution of slavery in America. They sometimes disagreed on ideology and strategy: Should abolitionists participate in the politics of a corrupt country? Was the Constitution a document that promised liberty for all or a tainted instrument that condoned slavery? But these abolitionists stood up to the power structure that sought to protect the right of property ownership in human beings.

Their work caused tremendous strife within American society in both the North and the South. Although the abolition movement was based in northern states, not all white northerners embraced freedom for blacks or held any thought of equality between blacks and whites. Indeed, even many of those who opposed slavery did not consider black people their equals. Those who opposed abolition or any hint of equality for black people often deployed physical violence against black residents and black and white abolitionists. In Canterbury, Connecticut, for example, Prudence Crandall, a white woman, and several black abolitionists established a boarding school for African American girls in 1833. The state legislature deemed it illegal to run a school for black students who came from outside the state, and an angry crowd of whites set the school on fire and then vandalized the building with clubs and iron bars. In 1835 William Lloyd Garrison barely escaped being tarred and feathered by an angry white mob in Boston.

In response to insistent calls from abolitionists to rid the country of slavery, proslavery advocates developed new defenses of slavery and designed political tactics aimed at keeping the institution in place. These arguments had first arisen in the wake of the American

Revolution as the country split geographically between free states and slave states, North and South. With new vehemence, its defenders argued that slavery was a positive good, not a moral failing tolerated only out of necessity; slavery was good for black people who were intended for nothing more, good for whites who benefitted from their labor, and good for the country. And, proslavery advocates raised religious defenses of slavery.

Supporters of slavery offered pseudo-scientific justifications as well; in 1851 Samuel A. Cartwright, a physician in New Orleans, sought to make forced labor and subordination of black people seem normal by diagnosing a disease in those slaves who attempted to escape from slavery. He called the disease "drapetomania," *drapeto* from the Greek for runaway slave, he said, and *mania* for madness or insanity. "The cause, in most cases, that induces the negro to run away from service," Cartwright wrote, "is as much a disease of the mind as any other species of mental alienation, and much more curable, as a general rule. With the advantages of proper medical advice, strictly followed, this troublesome practice that many negroes have of running away, can be almost entirely prevented, although the slaves be located on the borders of a free State, within a stone's throw of the abolitionists." In other words, according to Cartwright, slavery was the natural condition of black people and an enslaved person would have to be mentally ill to want to escape it.

On the political front, galvanizing their power in Congress, white southerners imposed a gag rule that prohibited Congress from taking up any antislavery petitions, thus diminishing the effectiveness of an important abolitionist strategy. Just as individual slave owners lived in fear of being killed by the people they owned, so too did these white elites fear a fatal attack by abolitionists on the entire system of slavery.

The issue of slavery was ubiquitous in the 1850s. Nearly every political matter raised the question of what to do about slavery and slaves. In 1853 Thomas Hart Benton, a Missouri senator, a slaveholder, and a member of the Free Soil Party that opposed the expansion of slavery but not slavery itself, came to the conclusion that no matter what policy a president pursued, Congress and the American people would interpret it in the light of its impact, real or potential, on slavery. The issue, according to Benton, was like the plague of frogs that God had inflicted on the Egyptians to convince them to release the Hebrews from bondage. "You could not look upon the table but there were frogs, you could not sit down at the banquet but there were frogs, you could not go to the bridal couch and lift the sheets but there were frogs! This black question," he said, was "forever on the table, on the nuptial couch, everywhere."

This "black question," as Benton called it, boiled down to the question of whether the United States would finally apply the words of the founding documents to all people, including African Americans, or whether it would continue to be a slave society with a large population of politically and socially powerless people in its midst. Southern states were very much afraid that the political power that had been written into the Constitution was threatened. Abolitionists wanted to end slavery, which would in fact greatly diminish the wealth and power of the Southern states. It is not simply in hindsight that historians speak now about the 1850s under the caption of "The Impending Crisis." Many people living at that time were aware that the country was on the verge of a crisis. At the Constitutional Convention in 1787, delegates from South Carolina and Georgia had insisted that they would not enter the Union if it threatened the economic institution on which they relied for survival. In the 1850s, slave owners realized that their institution faced its strongest threat ever. With sustained abolitionist agitation and heightened proslavery responses, America tumbled toward civil war.

One of the greatest sources of conflict concerned the growth and expansion of slavery. As the country grew geographically over the course of the nineteenth century—absorbing lands from the Louisiana Purchase in 1803; the area of Florida, purchased from Spain in 1817; lands from which Native Americans were forcibly removed in the 1830s; and land taken from Mexico in 1849 following the Mexican American War—so too did the number of people enslaved. When the American Revolution began in the 1770s, five hundred thousand slaves lived in America; in 1861 when the Civil War began, there were close to 4 million. Beginning in 1820 with the Missouri Compromise, Congress worked to maintain a numerical balance between slave states and free states because of the implications for representation in Congress. This compromise engineered by Henry Clay, Speaker of the House, allowed the Missouri territory that had been carved out of lands obtained with the Louisiana Purchase, to enter the Union as a slave state. Maine entered as a free state in which slavery would not be allowed. Now there would be twelve free states and twelve slave states. In anticipation of further expansion, Congress also prohibited slavery north of the southern border of Missouri, or the 36° 30′ latitude in the Louisiana territories. This compromise held for more than three decades. However, in the 1850s pro- and antislavery forces clashed over whether slavery should continue to expand with the country or be contained by the lines drawn by the Missouri Compromise.

By 1850, though, the Compromise was buckling under the weight of the nation's expansion in fulfillment of what some white men viewed as the country's manifest destiny to take control of all the land from the East Coast to California. Slavery was always in contention in these plans for expansion and ironically took center stage in 1849 when California applied for statehood, though there was no mention of slavery in its constitution. In fact, the territory wanted to exclude African Americans altogether. At the time there were fifteen free states and fifteen slave states, and admission of California as a free state would disturb that balance, granting more power in Congress to free states. New Mexico, a territory carved out of former Mexican lands, also signaled its intention to exclude slavery. Admission to statehood required congressional approval, but southern representatives feared complete loss of power.

After months of debate, Congress agreed to another compromise, one that had been proposed by Henry Clay. The compromise included four consequential provisions. First, California would enter the Union as a free state just as its citizens desired. Second, the remainder of the former Mexican territories would enter the Union under a plan of popular sovereignty in which citizens within those states would decide whether to permit slavery. Third, the domestic slave trade would be abolished in the District of Columbia, though slavery there would continue. And, fourth, Congress would enact a new and more stringent fugitive slave act.

The new fugitive slave law provoked fury on the part of abolitionists and succeeded in recruiting more northern whites to the antislavery clause. The Constitution provided for the return of fugitive slaves and Congress had enacted a fugitive slave law in 1793, but this new law galvanized antislavery sentiment. It allowed law enforcement officials to seize anyone suspected of being a fugitive and simply appear before a magistrate without any right to a trial by jury. The accused had no right to testify in any hearing, and after presentation of evidence by the alleged owner, the magistrate could order the alleged fugitive returned to slavery. Further, and most importantly for white northerners, the law provided punishment for any person who harbored or concealed a fugitive.

The author Harriet Beecher Stowe said that she had long been opposed to slavery, but it was passage of the 1850 Fugitive Slave Act that turned her into an abolitionist and led her to write *Uncle Tom's Cabin*, a novel in which she sought to expose slavery with all its physical violence, destruction of families, and sexual abuse of enslaved women. Published first in serial form in an abolitionist newspaper in 1851, the book was published in 1852. It sold hundreds of thousands of copies in America and England, and was translated into several languages. *Uncle Tom's Cabin* gained broad circulation and dispersed a message about the moral degeneration that accompanied slavery.

The 1854 trial of Anthony Burns in Boston influenced even more white northerners to oppose the fugitive slave law and slavery itself. Burns escaped from Richmond, Virginia, in March 1854, but when he wrote a letter to his brother, their owner intercepted it and, at the owner's behest, a commissioner in Boston issued a warrant for Burns's arrest as a fugitive from the service and labor of Charles Suttle. A group of abolitionists attempted unsuccessfully to free Burns from jail. When the magistrate ruled that Burns should be returned to slavery, hundreds of armed troops, including Marines sent in by President Franklin Pierce, marched Burns through the streets of Boston to a ship that took him back to Virginia. From her home in Salem, Massachusetts, where her father had sent her to avoid attending segregated schools in Philadelphia, the African American teacher Charlotte Forten wrote in her journal, "Our worse fears are realized, the decision was against poor Burns, and he has been sent back to a bondage worse, a thousand times worse than death. To-day Massachusetts has again been disgraced, again has she showed her submissions to the Slave Power; and Oh! With what deep sorrow do we think of what will doubtless be the fate of that poor man, when he is again consigned to the horrors of slavery."

Also in 1854, the federal Kansas-Nebraska Act, introduced by the Illinois politician Stephen Douglas, repealed the Missouri Compromise and made it possible for Kansas and Nebraska to enter the Union under a plan of popular sovereignty. Under the terms of the Missouri Compromise, both territories would have been free states. In what became known as "Bleeding Kansas," pro- and antislavery groups fought one another, each determined to populate the fertile Kansas territory with enough voters to influence the decision as to whether it would be a slave or free state. Several skirmishes took place, primarily involving attacks by proslavery men against free state men. On May 21, 1856, hundreds of proslavery men raided the town of Lawrence where many free state advocates had settled. They destroyed the printing presses and killed one man. In retaliation, John Brown, a white minister from Connecticut and his sons participated in a massacre that killed five proslavery whites. They reportedly hacked the men's bodies apart with swords.

The hostility and violence even made its way onto the Senate floor in May 1856. In a speech the Massachusetts senator Charles Sumner accused proslavery senators of cavorting with the harlot slavery. A few days later, Rep. Preston Brooks, a relative of one of the southern senators Sumner named, attacked Sumner in the Senate chambers, beating him on the head with a cane. It took Sumner nearly three years to recover from his injuries. Some whites in the South treated Brooks as a hero, sending him hundreds of canes.

In 1857 the Supreme Court stoked the divide between anti- and proslavery forces when it handed down its decision in the Dred Scott case. Scott had been enslaved by an army surgeon who took him and his wife from the slave state of Missouri into the Illinois and Wisconsin territories. Two years later they returned to Missouri. Scott sued his owner's widow for his freedom, claiming that because he had lived in a free territory for two years he was free then and should now forever be free. A jury of twelve white men in Missouri concluded that living in a free state and a free territory meant that Scott and his family were indeed free, but upon appeal the Missouri Supreme Court reversed the decision of the jury. Scott appealed to the U.S. Supreme Court that, in a 7–2 decision, denied his claim to freedom.

Writing for the majority, Chief Justice Roger Taney held that African Americans, even if free, could never be considered citizens of the United States and therefore had no standing to sue in federal court. This should have been enough for the court to decide not to hear the case, but Taney continued to render a much more far-reaching decision. He found that the federal government had no right under the Constitution to ban slavery in any territory or state, therefore the Missouri Compromise was void. And he said that the nation's founders had believed that blacks "had no rights which the white man was bound to respect." This provocative ruling pushed the country even closer to war. Abolitionists were irate about the Court's decision. As they saw it, the decision meant that slavery was now legal in any federal territory and raised a question of whether a state could choose to abolish slavery if the federal government could not.

In October 1859, John Brown, three of his sons, and nineteen other men, both black and white, raided the federal arsenal at Harpers Ferry, Virginia. They planned to seize arms from the arsenal and free enslaved people in Virginia. The men captured the arsenal in the middle of the night, but federal troops quickly surrounded them and killed several of the insurgents. Brown was captured, convicted, and sentenced to hang. In his last letter from prison, Brown said he did not fear his fate and invoked the language of the decision in the Dred Scott case: "Men cannot imprison, or chain, or hang the soul," he wrote. "I go joyfully in behalf of millions that 'have no right' that this great and glorious, this Christian republic, 'is bound to respect.'" He ended with an allusion to the American Revolution with its high ideals of freedom and equality, stating "Strange change in morals political, as well as Christian, since 1776." Brown thus became a martyr to fellow abolitionists.

As the tense and violent decade came to a close, the divided nation prepared for a presidential election. Abraham Lincoln ran as the nominee of the Republican party, which did not call for abolition but opposed expansion of slavery into new American states. When Lincoln was elected in November 1860 with no support from southern states, the crisis was no longer impending: it had arrived. Abolitionists, including Frederick Douglass, saw the election as a victory against the power of the slaveholding South even though Douglass thought Lincoln was not radical enough in his stance against slavery. Many whites in the South viewed Lincoln's election as humiliating, and they feared that the institution on which they depended would be destroyed. Southern leaders had threatened since the Constitutional Convention to disrupt the Union if the federal government interfered with the existence of slavery. Within a month after Lincoln's election, and before he was inaugurated, South Carolina, always the most stalwart defender of slavery, made the threats real and seceded from the Union. By February 1861, six other states—Mississippi, Florida, Alabama, Georgia, Louisiana, and Texas—also seceded to form the Confederate States of America.

The Confederacy protected the continued existence of slavery in its constitution, and on March 1861 Alexander Stephens, a congressman from Georgia and vice president of the Confederacy, gave a speech in which he laid out the causes for secession. Protection of the institution of slavery was at its heart. Earlier American statesmen, he opined, had thought slavery was somehow in violation of the laws of nature. To the contrary, he argued, the Confederacy's "corner-stone rests upon the great truth, that the negro is not equal to the white man; that slavery—subordination to the superior race—is his natural and normal condition. This, our new government, is the first, in the history of the world, based upon this great physical, philosophical, and moral truth." Stephens condemned as fanatics those people in the North who disagreed with his contentions, and argued that they suffered from a type of insanity that led them to engage in defective reasoning. He outright rejected any notion that blacks were equal to whites and therefore entitled to the same privileges. All members of the white race, he said, no matter how rich or poor, were equal under the law. But, "not so with the negro. Subordination is his place. He by nature, or by the curse against Canaan, is fitted for that condition which he occupies in our system." Stephens fortified his speech with the racist ideology that had developed over the centuries.

Although Stephens declared that peace was the Confederacy's only object, on April 12, 1861, Confederate troops attacked Fort Sumter, a federal fort located off the coast of South Carolina. The Confederacy argued that because of its location, the fort should now belong to the Confederacy. When Abraham Lincoln sent troops to defend Fort Sumter, Virginia, North Carolina, Arkansas, and Tennessee also seceded and joined the Confederacy. With the Confederate attack on Fort Sumter, the Civil War had begun.

As they had during the Revolutionary War, thousands of enslaved African Americans seized upon the displacement and disorder of war as an opportunity to gain freedom. One such move that had significant ramifications for both enslaved people and Union commanders for the duration of the war occurred at Fortress Monroe in Hampton, Virginia. In May 1861, just one month into the war, three enslaved men escaped and presented themselves to the Union general, Benjamin Butler. They informed him that their owners intended to send them South to build fortifications for the Confederacy. Their labor, they said, would be used against the Union. Butler concluded that as they were the property of the enemy he would treat them as contrabands of war. This placed the men in a limbo situation in which they were not quite free but were out of the grasp of their owners. When word seeped out, hundreds of enslaved people crowded across the bridge into the fort, seeking freedom. Within three months, nine hundred former slaves lived at Fortress Monroe. Such efforts at freedom met mixed results. In Missouri, Mattie Jackson, whose mother, Ellen Turner, had pasted a photograph of Abraham Lincoln on her wall, escaped and sought asylum with Union soldiers, but the soldiers returned her to their owners. Susie King Taylor, who as a young girl had surreptitiously attended a school with a black teacher, escaped and sailed from Savannah, Georgia, with a group of other slaves to a sea island, which the Union had captured.

9. Susie King Taylor learned to read and write as a child by sneaking into the home of a black woman who kept an illegal school for black children in Savannah. Taylor escaped slavery during the Civil War.

As people escaped and took on the status of contrabands of war, black abolitionists urged the president to permit African American men to enlist. They reasoned that these men should be allowed to fight for their own freedom and for the freedom of all African Americans. However, just as George Washington had resisted black enlistment, Lincoln, too, refused. This was a white man's war, he declared. But again, as Washington relented when his need for soldiers overwhelmed his fears of liberating slaves, Lincoln finally agreed to permit African American men to enlist at a time when white men from the North became less interested in fighting and after several Confederate victories. The official announcement came in the Emancipation Proclamation that Lincoln issued on January 1, 1863. Black men would be allowed to enlist, and enslaved men would gain their freedom upon enlistment. The Proclamation also provided that all slaves within territories under Confederate control were free; nonetheless, neither the president nor the Union Army had any power to enforce such a declaration.

Still, many African Americans interpreted the document as granting them freedom, and black abolitionists went into action to recruit black men to serve as soldiers. In one broadside they declared, "Men of Color To Arms! To Arms." The poster urged black men to challenge the label of cowardice that whites had imposed upon them. "A new era is upon us," it said. "For generations we have suffered under the horrors of slavery, outrage and wrong; our manhood has been denied, our citizenship blotted out, our souls seared and burned, our spirits cowed and crushed, and the hopes of the future of our race involved in doubt and darkness. But now our relations to the white race are changed. Now therefore is our most precious moment. Let us rush to arms."

Black men all over the country responded to the call to fight. Some came from the North and from Canada, but most came from southern states from among the ranks of enslaved men. Like Elijah Marrs and the twenty-five men who accompanied him

10. Thousands of African American men from the North and South, free and enslaved, enlisted in the Union Army during the Civil War. The men gained their freedom when they enlisted.

when he escaped and enlisted in the army in Camp Nelson, Kentucky, men stole away in the night, running in search of freedom. By the end of the war approximately 178,000 African American men had fought for the Union, 144,000 of them from the slave states. Most of these soldiers were former slaves. Not just men escaped during the war; women and children ran away as well, some moving into the contraband camps created to house the thousands of escaped slaves.

The war lasted until 1865, when on April 9 General Robert E. Lee surrendered the Confederate Army of Northern Virginia at the Appomattox Court House. Virginia was an apt place for the beginning of the end of the war and the imminent end of slavery because it was the place where, in 1619, twenty captive Africans had been purchased by English colonists. Slavery had been put into place and sustained over the course of two-and-a-half centuries, and it took a bloody war in which 750,000 people died to bring it to an end.

Within days of the Confederate surrender, John Wilkes Booth assassinated President Lincoln. In the aftermath of this event, many African Americans wondered if their freedom would survive his death. Two months before he died, Lincoln had approved the Joint Resolution of Congress submitting an amendment to the Constitution that would outlaw slavery. On December 6, 1865, after being ratified by the requisite number of states, the Thirteenth Amendment to the Constitution became law. It read: "Neither slavery nor involuntary servitude, except as a punishment for crime whereof the party shall have been duly convicted, shall exist within the United States, or any place subject to their jurisdiction." Slavery had finally come to an end in the United States of America.

Epilogue

The Thirteenth Amendment ended slavery, but it did not set things right. Over the course of slavery, whites had constructed beliefs, laws, policies, practices, and systems that designated blacks as inferior to whites and that separated blacks and whites socially. This racism, which enshrined privileges in whiteness, persisted in both the North and the South once slavery was abolished, and notions of black inferiority and white supremacy took on new shapes after black people were no longer slaves.

Following emancipation, African Americans waged profound struggles to make their freedom meaningful. Some set out on the roads or placed advertisements in newspapers to search for family members from whom they had been forcibly separated during slavery. Black communities, sometimes with help from the federal government's Freedmen's Bureau and missionary teachers from northern denominations, established schools for both children and adults. Freedpeople established independent churches free from white supervision, and they often housed schools in the sanctuaries. Some freedpeople established businesses. African Americans advocated in state legislatures for the right to serve on juries, the right to testify in court against whites, and most importantly, the right to vote.

> **Newspaper advertisement in which a former slave searched for family members sold during slavery**
>
> *Christian Recorder,* January 21, 1871
>
> INFORMATION WANTED of my father, Joshua Clarke, my mother Polly Clarke, my brother, Joshua and sister Kate. In our family there were four daughters and one son. I am the oldest daughter. I was sold about thirteen years ago, to Alabama. My father, mother, brothers and sisters were then living in Richmond, VA. Alice Mitchell, (Care of Rev. Levi Walker) Glenville, Barbour Co., Ala.
>
> Ministers will please read in their congregations.

African Americans faced immense challenges because many white southerners could not come to terms with having lost the war and fought hard to hold on to the pre–Civil War status quo. Not only had they lost an unpaid labor force but emancipation threatened the entire social system of racial hierarchy that their ancestors had put into place and which they had perpetuated. Many whites resisted the changes politically as well as with violence. The end of the war saw the birth of the Ku Klux Klan, the Red Shirts, and other extralegal terrorist organizations that intimidated, threatened, and murdered African Americans who dared to organize politically or even to teach school.

From 1867 to 1877 during the period of Congressional or Radical Reconstruction, African Americans made political gains as the U.S. government kept troops in southern states and the Freedmen's Bureau provided assistance to freedpeople, even as it endeavored to keep them working on plantations to produce the crops on which much of the nation's economy relied. Congress passed, and in 1868 the states ratified, the Fourteenth Amendment to the Constitution that granted citizenship to African Americans and promised equal protection under the law.

In 1870 the states ratified the Fifteenth Amendment that gave black men the right to vote. During Reconstruction, African American men held elected offices in state legislatures and in the U.S. Congress, but following the controversial presidential election of Rutherford B. Hayes in 1876, the federal government withdrew troops from southern states, leaving African Americans completely under the control of white-ruled governments. There would be no protection for blacks in the South.

Southern state legislatures began to essentially extinguish African Americans' right to vote and put in place systems of segregation that severely circumscribed African Americans' economic,

---

Excerpts from the Fourteenth and Fifteenth Amendments to the Constitution

AMENDMENT XIV

Passed by Congress June 13, 1866. Ratified July 9, 1868.

Section 1. All persons born or naturalized in the United States, and subject to the jurisdiction thereof, are citizens of the United States and of the State wherein they reside. No State shall make or enforce any law which shall abridge the privileges or immunities of citizens of the United States; nor shall any State deprive any person of life, liberty, or property, without due process of law; nor deny to any person within its jurisdiction the equal protection of the laws.

AMENDMENT XV

Passed by Congress February 26, 1869. Ratified February 3, 1870.

Section 1. The right of citizens of the United States to vote shall not be denied or abridged by the United States or by any State on account of race, color, or previous condition of servitude—

political, and social options. By the end of the 1890s, Jim Crow laws in the South discriminated against blacks in public schools, public transportation, and public accommodations, and designated a subordinate place for African Americans. The retrenchment only continued when in 1896 the U.S. Supreme Court in *Plessy v. Ferguson* upheld the constitutionality of what it called, "separate but equal" treatment for African Americans. From the end of the Civil War to the 1950s, more than 6 million black southerners moved north and west to escape what was, in reality, dramatically unequal treatment and oppression in southern states. Northern and western states were no panacea either, as they often had policies and practices that discriminated against African Americans, but they offered some relief from the relentless racism of the South.

It was not until the modern civil rights movement of the 1940s, '50s and '60s, a period that some have called the Second Emancipation or the Second Reconstruction, that these discriminatory laws and practices finally began to give way. Still, throughout the society white privilege survived, and in some quarters white supremacy remains a thriving ideology. For many African Americans, struggles for equality, justice, and fairness continue into the twenty-first century.

References

Chapter 1: The Atlantic slave trade

Samuel Crowther, *The Narrative of Samuel Ajayi Crowther*. In *Africa Remembered: Narratives by West Africans from the Era of the Slave Trade*, ed. Philip D. Curtin (Madison: University of Wisconsin Press, 1967).

Ottobah Cugoano, *Narrative of the Enslavement of Ottobah Cugoano, a Native of Africa*; Published by Himself, in the Year 1787, quoted in Curtin, *Africa Remembered*.

Philip D. Curtin, ed., *Africa Remembered: Narratives by West Africans from the Era of the Slave Trade* (Madison: University of Wisconsin Press, 1967).

David Brion Davis, *Inhuman Bondage: The Rise and Fall of Slavery in the New World* (New York: Oxford University Press, 2006).

Elizabeth Donnan, *Documents Illustrative of the History of the Slave Trade to America*, vol. 1 (Washington, DC: Carnegie Institution of Washington, 1930–35).

David Eltis, *The Rise of African Slavery in the Americas* (New York: Cambridge University Press, 2000).

David Eltis, "The Volume and Structure of the Transatlantic Slave Trade: A Reassessment," *William and Mary Quarterly* 58, no. 1 (2006): 13–34.

David Eltis and David Richardson, eds., *Extending the Frontiers: Essays on the Transatlantic Slave Trade Database* (New Haven, CT: Yale University Press, 2010).

David Eltis et al., *Voyages: The Trans-Atlantic Slave Trade Database* (Emory University; The University of Hull; Universidade

Federal do Rio de Janerio; Victoria University of Wellington).
http://www.slavevoyages.org/tast/index.faces

Alexander Falconbridge, *An Account of the Slave Trade on the Coast of Africa* (London, 1788).

Michael Gomez, *Reversing Sail: A History of the African Diaspora* (New York: Cambridge University Press, 2005).

April Lee Hatfield, *Atlantic Virginia: Intercolonial Relations in the Seventeenth Century* (Philadelphia: University of Pennsylvania Press, 2004).

Herbert S. Klein, *The Atlantic Slave Trade* (New York: Cambridge University Press, 2010).

Lisa A. Lindsay, *Captives as Commodities: The Transatlantic Slave Trade* (Upper Saddle River, NJ: Pearson, Prentice Hall, 2008).

Paul E. Lovejoy, *Transformations in Slavery: A History of Slavery in Africa* (Cambridge: Cambridge University Press, 2000).

Malyn Newitt, ed., *The Portuguese in West Africa, 1415-1670* (New York: Cambridge University Press, 2010).

John Newton, *The Journal of a Slave Trader (John Newton 1750-1754) with Newton's Thoughts Upon the African Slave Trade*, ed. Bernard Martin and Mark Spurrell (London: Epworth Press, 1962).

David Northrup, ed., *The Atlantic Slave Trade*, Problems in World History Series (Lexington, MA: D. C. Heath, 1994).

Orlando Patterson, *Slavery and Social Death: A Comparative Study* (Cambridge, MA: Harvard University Press, 1982).

Peter Russell, *Prince Henry "The Navigator": A Life* (New Haven, CT: Yale University Press, 2000).

A. J. R. Russell-Wood, *A World on the Move: The Portuguese in Africa, Asia, and America, 1415-1808* (Manchester, UK: Carcanet Press, 1992).

Stephanie Smallwood, *Saltwater Slavery: A Middle Passage from Africa to American Diaspora* (Cambridge, MA: Harvard University Press, 2007).

John Thornton, *Africa and Africans in the Making of the Atlantic World, 1400-1800* (1992; repr. New York: Cambridge University Press, 1998).

Chapter 2: Putting slavery into place

Ira Berlin, *Many Thousands Gone: The First Two Centuries of Slavery in North America* (Cambridge, MA: Harvard University Press, 1998).

Converse D. Clowse, *Economic Beginnings in Colonial South Carolina, 1670–1730* (Columbia: University of South Carolina Press, 1971).

Alan Gallay, ed., *Indian Slavery in Colonial America* (Lincoln: University of Nebraska Press, 2009).

Lorenzo Johnston Greene, *The Negro in Colonial New England* (New York: Atheneum, 1974).

Leslie Harris, *In the Shadow of Slavery: African Americans in New York City, 1626–1863* (Chicago: University of Chicago Press, 2003).

Graham Russell Hodges, *Root and Branch: African Americans in New York and East Jersey* (Chapel Hill: University of North Carolina Press, 1999).

Winthrop Jordan, *White over Black: American Attitudes Toward the Negro, 1550–1812* (Chapel Hill: University of North Carolina Press, 1968).

Susan Kingsbury, ed., *The Records of the Virginia Company of London*, vols. 2 and 4 (Washington, DC: Government Printing Office, 1935).

Allan Kulikoff, *Tobacco and Slaves: The Development of Southern Cultures in the Chesapeake, 1680–1800* (Chapel Hill: University of North Carolina Press, 1986).

Jane Landers, *Black Society in Spanish Florida* (Urbana: University of Illinois Press, 1999).

Elise Lemire, *Black Walden: Slavery and Its Aftermath in Concord, Massachusetts* (Philadelphia: University of Pennsylvania Press, 2009).

C. S. Manegold, *Ten Hills Farm: The Forgotten History of Slavery in the North* (Princeton, NJ: Princeton University Press, 2010).

Edgar J. McManus, *A History of Negro Slavery in New York* (Syracuse, NY: Syracuse University Press, 1966).

Edmund S. Morgan, *American Slavery, American Freedom* (New York: W. W. Norton, 1975).

Anthony S. Parent Jr., *Foul Means: The Formation of a Slave Society in Virginia, 1660–1740* (Chapel Hill, NC: Omohundro Institute of Early American History, 2003).

Robert H. Romer, *Slavery in the Connecticut Valley of Massachusetts* (Chapel Hill: University of North Carolina Press, 2009).

Captain John Smith, *Writings with Other Narratives of Roanoke, Jamestown, and the First English Settlement of America* (New York: Penguin Putnam, Inc., 1984).

Julia Floyd Smith, *Slavery and Rice Culture in Low Country Georgia, 1750–1860* (Knoxville: University of Tennessee Press, 1985).

William Thorndale, "The Virginia Census of 1619," *Magazine of Virginia Genealogy* 33 (1995): 155–70.

John Winthrop, *Journal of John Winthrop*, entry of February 26, 1638, The John Harvard Library Series (Cambridge, MA: Belknap Press, 1997).

Betty Wood, *Slavery in Colonial Georgia, 1730–1775* (Athens: University of Georgia Press, 1984).

Peter H. Wood, *Black Majority: Negroes in Colonial South Carolina from 1670 through the Stono Rebellion* (New York: W. W. Norton, 1974).

Chapter 3: The work of slavery

Michelle Adams, *Boone Hall Plantation* (Charleston, SC: Arcadia Publishing, 2008).

John F. Baker Jr., *The Washingtons of Wessyngton Plantation: Stories of My Family's Journey to Freedom* (New York: Simon and Schuster, 2009).

Ira Berlin, *Many Thousands Gone: The First Two Centuries of Slavery in North America* (Cambridge, MA: Harvard University Press, 1998).

Daina Ramey Berry, *"Swing the Sickle for the Harvest Is Ripe": Gender and Slavery in Antebellum Georgia* (Urbana: University of Illinois Press, 2007).

James O. Breeden, *Advice Among Masters: The Ideal in Slave Management in the Old South* (Westport, CT: Greenwood Press, 1980).

Converse D. Clowse, *Economic Beginnings in Colonial South Carolina, 1670–1730* (Columbia: University of South Carolina Press, 1971).

David Brion Davis, *Inhuman Bondage: The Rise and Fall of Slavery in the New World* (New York: Oxford University Press, 2006).

Ralph Betts Flanders, *Plantation Slavery in Georgia* (Cos Cob, CT: John E. Edwards, 1967).

Henry Louis Gates, "Mister Jefferson and the Trials of Phillis Wheatley" (speech), National Endowment for the Humanities, 2002 Jefferson Lecture. http://www.neh.gov/about/awards/jefferson-lecture/henry-louis-gates-jr-lecture.

Lorenzo Johnston Greene, *The Negro in Colonial New England* (New York: Atheneum, 1974).

Robert Gudmestad, *Steamboats and the Rise of the Cotton Kingdom* (Baton Rouge: Louisiana State University Press, 2011).

Leslie M. Harris, *In the Shadow of Slavery: African Americans in New York City, 1626–1863* (Chicago: University of Chicago Press, 2003).

Graham Russell Hodges, *Root and Branch: African Americans in New York and East Jersey* (Chapel Hill: University of North Carolina Press, 1999).

Jessee Holland, *Black Men Built the Capitol: Discovering African American History in and Around Washington, D.C.* (Guilford, CT: Globe Pequot Press, 2007).

Thomas Jefferson, *Notes on the State of Virginia,* ed. David Waldstreicher (Boston: Bedford/St. Martin's, 2002).

David Koburn, *The Black Minority in Early New York* (Albany: SUNY Press, 1971).

Ronald L. Lewis, *Coal, Iron and Slaves: Industrial Slavery in Maryland and Virginia, 1715–1865* (Westport, CT: Greenwood Press, 1979).

Edgar J. McManus, *A History of Negro Slavery in New York* (Syracuse, NY: Syracuse University Press, 1966).

Suanne Gehring Schnittman, "Slavery in Virginia's Urban Tobacco Industry, 1840–1860," (PhD diss., University of Rochester, 1987).

Kenneth M. Stampp, *The Peculiar Institution: Slavery in the Ante-Bellum South* (1956; repr. New York: Vintage Books, 1989).

Robert S. Starobin, *Industrial Slavery in the Old South* (New York: Oxford University Press, 1970).

Chapter 4: Struggles for control

Mia Bay, *The White Image in the Black Mind: African American Ideas about White People, 1830–1925* (New York: Oxford University Press, 2000).

Ira Berlin, *Many Thousands Gone: The First Two Centuries of Slavery in North America* (Cambridge, MA: Harvard University Press, 1998).

James O. Breeden, *Advice Among Masters: The Ideal in Slave Management in the Old South* (Westport, CT: Greenwood Press, 1980).

James Curry, "Narrative of James Curry, a Fugitive Slave" (originally printed in *the Liberator,* January 10, 1840), in *Slave Testimony: Two Centuries of Letters, Speeches, Interviews, and Autobiographies,* ed. John Blassingame (Baton Rouge: Louisiana State University Press, 1997).

Frederick Douglass, *Narrative of the Life of Frederick Douglass, an American Slave, Written by Himself*, ed. David Blight (Boston: Bedford/St. Martin's, 2003).

Drew Gilpin Faust, *James Henry Hammond and the Old South: A Design for Mastery* (Baton Rouge: Louisiana State University Press, 1982).

William Goodell, *The American Slave Code in Theory and Practice: Its Distinctive Features Shown by Its Statutes, Judicial Decisions, and Illustrative Facts* (Whitefish, MT: Kessinger Publications, 2007).

Sally Greene, "State v. Mann Exhumed," *North Carolina Law Review* 87, no. 3 (March 2009): 701–56.

Harriet Jacobs, *Incidents in the Life of a Slave Girl*, ed. Jean Fagan Yellin (Cambridge, MA: Harvard University Press, 1987).

Albert J. Raboteau, *Slave Religion: The "Invisible Institution" in the Antebellum South* (New York: Oxford University Press, 2004).

James C. Scott, *Domination and the Arts of Resistance: Hidden Transcripts* (New Haven, CT: Yale University Press, 1990).

David Walker, *Appeal to the Coloured Citizens of the World*, ed. Sean Wilentz (New York: Hill and Wang, 1965).

Heather Andrea Williams, *Self-Taught: African American Education in Slavery and Freedom* (Chapel Hill: University of North Carolina Press, 2005).

Peter Wood, *Black Majority: Negroes in Colonial South Carolina from 1670 through the Stono Rebellion* (New York: W. W. Norton, 1996).

Chapter 5: Surviving slavery

Sylviane A. Diouf, *Servants of Allah: African Muslims Enslaved in the Americas* (New York: New York University Press, 1998).

Frederick Douglass, *Life and Times of Frederick Douglass.* Quotes re: grandmother are from *Life and Times,* 29–30 (Boston: De Wolfe and Fiske, 1982).

Frederick Douglass, *Narrative of the Life of Frederick Douglass, an American Slave, Written by Himself*, ed. David Blight (Boston: Bedford/St. Martin's, 2003).

Paul Finkleman, *Defending Slavery: Proslavery Thought in the Old South* (Boston: Bedford/St. Martin's, 2003).

David R. Goldfield, "Black Life in Old South Cities," in *Before Freedom Came: African-American Life in the Antebellum South*, ed. Edward D. C. Campbell Jr., with Kym S. Rice (Charlottesville: University of Virginia Press, 1991).

Michael A. Gomez, *Exchanging Our Country Marks: The Transformation of African Identities in the Colonial Antebellum South* (Chapel Hill: University of North Carolina Press, 1998).

Herbert Gutman, *The Black Family in Slavery and Freedom, 1750–1925* (New York: Pantheon Books, 1976).

Leslie Harris, *In the Shadow of Slavery: African Americans in New York City, 1626–1863* (Chicago: University of Chicago Press, 2003).

Hinton Rowan Helper, *The Impending Crisis of the South: How to Meet It.* (1857).

Samuel S. Hill, Charles H. Lippy, and Charles Reagan Wilson, eds., *Encyclopedia of Religion in the South* (Macon, GA: Mercer University Press, 2005).

Charles Joyner, *Down by the Riverside: A South Carolina Slave Community* (Urbana: University of Illinois Press, 1984).

Theresa Singleton, "The Archaeology of Slave Life," *Before Freedom Came: African American Life in the Antebellum South*, ed. Edward D. C. Campbell, Jr., and Kym S. Rice (Charlottesville: University of Virginia Press, 1991).

Kenneth Stampp, *The Peculiar Institution: Slavery in the Ante-bellum South* (New York: Vintage Books, 1989).

Heather Andrea Williams, *Help Me to Find My People: The African American Search for Family Lost in Slavery* (Chapel Hill: University of North Carolina Press, 2012).

Chapter 6: Taking slavery apart

William E. Cain, *William Lloyd Garrison and the Fight Against Slavery* (Boston: Bedford/St. Martin's, 1995).

David Brion Davis, "The Emergence of Immediatism in British and American Antislavery Thought," *Mississippi Valley Historical Review* 49, no. 2 (1962): 209–30.

David Brion Davis, *The Problem of Slavery in the Age of Revolution, 1770–1823* (New York: Oxford University Press, 1999).

Paul Finkleman, *Defending Slavery: Proslavery Thought in the Old South* (Boston: Bedford/St. Martin's, 2003).

Philip S. Foner, ed., "A New Nation—With Slavery," in *History of Black Americans: From Africa to the Emergence of the Cotton Kingdom* (Westport, CT: Greenwood Press, 1975).

Elizabeth Heyrick, "Immediate, Not Gradual Abolition." Boston, 1838.

James Oliver Horton and Lois E. Horton, *In Hope of Liberty: Culture, Community and Protest Among Northern Free Blacks, 1700–1860* (New York: Oxford University Press, 1997).

Joanne Pope Melish, *Disowning Slavery: Gradual Emancipation and "Race" in New England, 1780–1860* (Ithaca, NY: Cornell University Press, 1998).

Gary B. Nash and Jean R. Soderlund, *Freedom by Degrees: Emancipation in Pennsylvania and Its Aftermath* (New York: Oxford University Press, 1991).

Benjamin Quarles, *The Negro in the American Revolution* (Chapel Hill: University of North Carolina Press, 1996).

Jean R. Soderlund, *Quakers and Slavery: A Divided Spirit* (Princeton, NJ: Princeton University Press, 1985).

Josiah H. Temple, *History of Framingham, Massachusetts, 1640–1880* (published by the Town of Framingham, MA, 1887).

David Walker, *Appeal to the Coloured Citizens of the World*, ed. Sean Wilentz (New York: Hill and Wang, 1965).

Heather Andrea Williams, *Self-Taught: African American Education in Slavery and Freedom* (Chapel Hill: University of North Carolina Press, 2005).

Further reading

Slavery

Bishir, Catherine. *African American Artisans in New Bern, North Carolina, 1770–1900*. Chapel Hill: University of North Carolina Press, 2013.

Douglass, Frederick. *Narrative of the Life of Frederick Douglass*. Edited by David Blight. Boston: Bedford/St. Martin's, 2003.

Fett, Sharla M. *Working Cures: Healing, Health, and Power on Southern Slave Plantations*. Chapel Hill: University of North Carolina Press, 2002.

Franklin, John Hope, and Loren Schweninger. *Runaway Slaves: Rebels on the Plantation*. New York: Oxford University Press, 1999.

Frey, Sylvia R., and Betty Wood. *Come Shouting to Zion: African American Protestantism in the American South and British Caribbean to 1830*. Chapel Hill: University of North Carolina Press, 1998.

Gutman, Herbert. *The Black Family in Slavery and Freedom, 1750–1925*. New York: Vintage, 1976.

Johnson, Walter. *Soul by Soul: Life Inside the Antebellum Slave Market*. Cambridge, MA: Harvard University Press, 1999.

Jordan, Winthrop D. *White over Black: American Attitudes Toward the Negro, 1550–1812*. Chapel Hill: University of North Carolina Press, 1968.

Morgan, Jennifer L. *Laboring Women: Reproduction and Gender in New World Slavery*. Philadelphia: University of Pennsylvania Press, 2004.

Penningroth, Dylan. *The Claims of Kinfolk: African American Property and Community in the Nineteenth-Century South*. Chapel Hill: University of North Carolina Press, 2003.

Rediker, Marcus. *The Slave Ship: A Human History*. New York: Viking, 2007.

Schwartz, Marie Jenkins. *Born in Bondage: Growing Up Enslaved in the Antebellum South*. Cambridge, MA: Harvard University Press, 2001.

White, Deborah Gray. *Ar'n't I a Woman? Female Slaves in the Plantation South*. New York: W. W. Norton, 1999.

Reconstruction

DuBois, W. E. B. *Black Reconstruction in America: An Essay toward a History of the Part which Black Folk Played in the Attempt to Reconstruct Democracy in America, 1860–1880*. New York: Oxford University Press, 2007.

Foner, Eric. *Reconstruction: America's Unfinished Revolution, 1863–1877*. New York: Harper and Row, 1988.

Glymph, Thavolia. *Out of the House of Bondage: The Transformation of the Plantation Household*. New York: Cambridge University Press, 2008.

Litwack, Leon F. *Been in the Storm So Long: The Aftermath of Slavery*. New York: Knopf, 1979.

Websites for primary sources on American slavery

American Memory—The Library of Congress
http://memory.loc.gov/ammem/browse/ListSome
    .php?category=African%20American%20History

The Avalon Project: Documents in Law, History and Diplomacy
http://avalon.law.yale.edu/

**Documenting the American South. University of North Carolina
    at Chapel Hill**
http://docsouth.unc.edu/

**History Matters—Graduate Center, City University of New York
    and George Mason University**
http://historymatters.gmu.edu/search.php?function=find

**"John Brown: The Abolitionist and His Legacy." Gilder Lehrman
    Institute of American History**
http://www.gilderlehrman.org/sites/default/files/swf/jbrown/index.php

Massachusetts Constitution, Judicial Review, and Slavery
http://www.mass.gov/courts/sjc/constitution-slavery-e.html

**"Slavery and the Making of the University." University of North
    Carolina at Chapel Hill**
http://www2.lib.unc.edu/mss/exhibits/slavery/index.html

"Slavery in New York"—New-York Historical Society
http://www.slaveryinnewyork.org/

Voyages: The Atlantic Slave Trade Database (Emory University (US), The University of Hull (UK), Universidade Federal do Rio de Janeiro (Brazil), Victoria University of Wellington (New Zealand)
http://www.slavevoyages.org/tast/index.faces

Index

Index